Seven Things that can "Make or Break" a Sweater™

Techniques and Tips for Hand Knitters

Margaret E. Fisher

First printing, August 2008
Second printing, December 2008

ISBN 978-0-9814986-0-7

Book design and layout: Naylor Design, Inc.
Book cover: Naylor Design, Inc.
Photography: Rob Kibler—swatch and technique photographs; author photograph
                Fredde Lieberman—cover and sweater photographs
Illustrations: Rob Kibler

Vanduki Press
P.O. Box 113
Cabin John, MD 20818

web site: www.fisher-designs.com
email: margaret@fisher-designs.com

Printed by Friesens in Manitoba, Canada

To my Aunt Gene—Eugenie Eaton. She was independent and open-minded, one of my biggest supporters, and like a mother to me. She also taught me to knit. I love her and miss her.

Acknowledgements

Like you, I have read the acknowledgements sections in many different books. I have always wondered why so many people are mentioned. How many people can it possibly take for one author to write a book? Well, I have written a book, and now I know. It takes a lot, and I want to mention all who have helped me. My sincerest thanks to:

Mary Marik, who edited this book. She is a professional editor, a knitter, and a published knitwear designer. Editing a book is a huge job, and I want to say a huge thank you for all you have done. I enjoyed working with you—it was a wonderful experience—and I appreciate your careful and thoughtful editing.

Charlotte Quiggle, a knitting professional who is known for her articles, knitwear designs, and technical editing expertise. She did a superb job of editing my patterns. Charlotte, it was a pleasure to work with you. Your great sense of humor made it fun, and I learned a lot from you.

Debra Naylor, who artistically and skillfully designed this book. She is a master of book design, combining amazing creativity with practicality. I am thankful for her beautiful work and excellent guidance. And Diane Guy, who contributed to the book design process. Debra and Diane are knitters, and their knowledge of my subject-matter was extremely helpful.

The very talented Fredde Lieberman, photographer of the garments, who knows how to shoot textured fabrics and make them pop! I first saw Fredde "in action" a number of years ago when he gave a workshop to my fiber guild about how to photograph artwork. I am pleased to have his artistry in my book. Thanks to him, my readers will be able to see every stitch in every sweater.

My husband, Rob Kibler, swatch and hand photographer, illustrator, computer guru, and proofreader extraordinaire. This book would not have happened without your superior skills, your calming effect on me, and your realistic outlook on everything. You believed in this book from my very first mention of it and have consistently offered encouragement. Without you, I could not have followed my dream. Your love and support mean the world to me.

Alexandra Barnard, who modeled the sweaters in this book. I was overjoyed the day Alex stopped by my studio to try on the sweaters. They fit her beautifully and she wears them so well. A graduate of Gettysburg College, Alex is pursuing a career in theater production and management. She is a lovely young woman, charming and kind. Alex, thanks for your help and for making my sweaters look great.

Peggy Jo Wells of Brown Sheep Company, Stephanie Richards of Cascade Yarns, and Paul Nichols of Mission Falls who generously provided yarn for the sweaters in this book.

The test knitters who gave me valuable feedback on my written instructions: Tish Davidson, Karen Fisher, Sandie Isbister, Ann Lambert, Audrey Lewis, and Ellen Torke. They embody the generosity and enthusiasm of knitters everywhere. Their dedication, knitting skills, and attention to detail are greatly appreciated.

Bobbi Dunn, Renie Yoshida Grohl, Gayle Roehm, and Susan White, experienced and knowledgeable knitters, who did a terrific job of proofreading my final draft. When I asked for help, each of them said "yes" immediately. Thank you.

Ellen Torke, one of my dearest and closest friends, who encouraged, supported, and listened to me throughout the writing of this book, just as she has over the past 30 years. Friendship is one of the most precious things in life, and I will always treasure ours.

Karen Fisher, my sister and friend. I am most grateful for your efforts, not only on this book, but in the many other ways you have helped me over the years.

Candace Eisner Strick and Judy Pascale, two incredibly talented designers and dear friends. You are inspirations. We have shared good times in many places and it's been fun. Thanks for the excellent advice and for believing in me.

Cat Bordhi, who generously shared information about self-publishing at her 2007 Visionary Retreat, and who gave me the knowledge and confidence to self-publish this book. And all of the attendees of that retreat—I'm not sure I should name names but you know who you are. I appreciate your feedback, interest, excitement, and support.

Friends, fellow knitters, designers, and artists who gave me advice and encouragement, kindly shared information, and put me in touch with others who were able to help me: Janet Barnard, Carol Breitner, Chris de Longpré, Chrissy Gardiner, Roz Houseknecht, Kathie Power Johnson, Joyce Keister, Betsy Kulamer, Diane Kelly, Debra Lee, Audrey Sherins, Myrna Stahman, Janet Szabo, and Jill Wolcott.

The Master Hand Knitting Program of The Knitting Guild Association (TKGA) and Jean Lampe who reviewed two of my three submissions to that program. I thought I knew lots about knitting, but I learned how much I didn't know when I went through the program. I am extremely grateful to Jean, whose critiques of my submissions were invaluable. She became my mentor in the early years after I received my Master Knitter certification, and she recommended me for positions that put me on the path I'm following today.

My many students, who have taught me more than they can imagine. One of the joys of teaching is learning from my students. And those students who have asked me again and again: "When are you going to write a book?" Your encouragement and gentle nudging have been helpful. Here is that book.

Kiwi and Van Gogh, my feline companions, and Mandu, now gone but always in my heart. In return for your luxurious life of sleeping, playing, eating, and being petted whenever you want, you give me much happiness, many laughs, and a different perspective on everything, including knitting. To you, high-end yarn is merely a plaything and handknit sweaters are perfect cat beds.

Contents

Preface

Knitting technique is important. Whether you're making a trendy, fashionable sweater, a wearable-art piece, or a classic raglan pullover, the same techniques will help you produce a beautifully handmade garment. These techniques are little things, or details, that have a huge impact on the appearance of a garment. They make the difference between a sweater that looks well made and one that doesn't.

Seven things—techniques and methods—can greatly affect the appearance of a handknit sweater: the smooth or bumpy side of the cast-on edge on the public side of the garment, the placement and type of increases used in ribbing, slanting decreases, invisible increases, blocking, picking up stitches for bands, and buttonholes.

Each chapter in this book focuses on one of these topics. This book reviews the techniques, most of which can be found in other books, but it also provides tips and hints for achieving good results. After I explain the "how" of the techniques, I discuss the "when and where" of using the techniques. The reader will understand why these particular techniques work well. All the techniques are described as they are used in sweaters, although they can be used in many other types of knitting projects, too.

The chapters take the reader step by step through the process of making a sweater. A baby sweater pattern is provided as a tutorial project. The pattern, on page 79, is divided into sections that correspond to each chapter. You will be able to read a chapter, then work a section of the sweater that uses the technique just covered.

A Class Becomes a Book

This book is based on a class I taught first in 2000 and have taught many times since—at knitting conventions and at shops and for guilds across the country. I developed the workshop for two reasons.

In 1997 I completed the Master Hand Knitting Program of The Knitting Guild Association (TKGA). It is a comprehensive, educational, self-study program that covers many aspects of knitting. In the program's three levels, I learned much about technique, stitch patterns, different types of knitting, reference sources, and design. Shortly after I received my Master Hand Knitter certification, I was asked to become a member of the Master Hand Knitting Committee, the committee that reviews the submissions to the program. Later I became the co-chair of the committee.

In the late 1990s, I thought about putting together a class that covered some of the techniques I was critiquing and often reviewing with the program participants. I was also teaching at a local shop at the time, and I noticed that many of my students often asked questions about certain techniques: What's a good buttonhole? Which way do decreases slant and why should I care? How do I pick up stitches so the front band doesn't flare? These were the same techniques I was reviewing and critiquing for the Master Hand Knitting Program. Voila! A class was born. And now, at the urging of many knitters who have taken my class, I have turned it into a book.

My Knitting Philosophy

Knitting is about choices. There often isn't a right or wrong. Different approaches or methods can be used to achieve a result. However, a particular method or technique may look best or work best in a certain situation. In this book, I will show you techniques that work, and I'll help you understand why they work and why they look good. I won't say, "This is the only way to do it and you must always do it this way." My goal is to give you the knowledge and understanding of the techniques or "the tools in your toolbox" so you can make choices in your knitting.

Many knitters joke about the "knitting police" who enforce the "rules" of knitting and tell us whether our work is OK or not. But we all know the knitting police don't exist. Your friends may want a closer look at your sweaters. They may even grab the edge of your sweater while you are wearing it and turn it over to check the inside. But unless you are selling your work, entering it in a juried competition, or submitting it for review such as to the Master Hand Knitting Program, no one will scrutinize it in the detailed way you will.

Even if no one else looks closely, some knitters want the sweater to be perfect, with the inside looking as great as the outside. I must confess that I am one of those people. But I understand that not everyone is like me. I may think a particular technique looks best, but another knitter may prefer something else. If you disagree with me, that's OK. The real bottom line is that in your sweater, you get to decide what looks best and what works for you. As I said, knitting is about choices.

Skill Level

This book is for knitters with advanced-beginner-level skills. It assumes the reader knows how to cast on, bind off, work a knit stitch, work a purl stitch, make and measure a gauge swatch, read written instructions, and interpret basic knitting abbreviations and terminology. It also assumes that the reader has made a few projects, preferably garments, and as a result understands the overall construction of clothing, including shaping, finishing, and assembling. With that said, relatively new knitters and people who have knit for many years may learn new things in this book. The advanced-beginner knitter will learn a number of techniques that work and will understand why they do. For longtime knitters who have not taken classes on technique or read knitting reference sources, the book may provide new insight on familiar techniques and topics.

Please Write in This Book

You may not like to write in books, but I am going to encourage you to write in this one. Go ahead and jot your notes next to the descriptions of the techniques. Get the wording down in your own language, the way you understand it, because then you'll be able to review the instructions for a technique and do it again later. For instance, if an instruction says, "move the needle from right to left" but you think of this maneuver as "counterclockwise," then by all means write it down that way. I hope this is a resource you will use frequently, so please write in this book.

Have Fun

Knitting a sweater is a great experience. This creative process can be meditative and relaxing, and when we're finished, we have something wonderful to wear. Mastering these seven things will increase your skill set and, as a result, build your confidence. You will enjoy the knitting process even more, and you will be pleased with the results. I hope you have fun knitting and wearing sweaters!

Seven Things

Chapter 1

Cast-On Edge

Let's start at the beginning by talking about the cast-on edge of a sweater. As soon as you cast on for a sweater project, you have a decision to make: Which side of the cast on will be on the right side—the public side—of this sweater?

This is completely your decision, so be sure to make that decision consciously and thoughtfully. Let's talk about your choices and how you decide.

Examine the Cast On You Usually Use

Look at one of your hand-knit projects—a sweater, scarf, hat, purse, or anything else that you have knit. Examine the cast-on edge on the right side of the fabric. Now look at the wrong side. Do you notice that one side looks smooth and the other side looks bumpy? Most of the cast ons that are taught to beginning knitters, like the long-tail cast on (see Techniques) and the cable cast on (see Chapter 7), have a smooth side and a bumpy side.

Some cast ons do not have a smooth side and a bumpy side, but I am going to make the following grand, sweeping statement: *Most of the cast ons that most of us use most of the time have one side that's smooth and one side that's bumpy.*

Smooth or Bumpy?

This leads to the question: Which side of the cast-on edge goes on the public side (the right side or the outside) of the sweater? Smooth? Or bumpy? Either answer is correct because you, the knitter, get to decide.

Smooth side of long-tail cast on (K1 P1 rib swatch).

Some knitters prefer to have the smooth side of the cast on appear on the public side when the stitch pattern following the cast on has a smooth look—when the stitch pattern has prominent knit stitches, as in ribbing and stockinette stitch. Some knitters prefer to have the bumpy side of the cast on appear on the public side when the stitch pattern following the cast on has a bumpy look—when the stitch pattern has prominent

Bumpy side of long-tail cast on (K1 P1 rib swatch).

purl stitches, as in garter stitch, seed stitch, and reverse stockinette stitch. But if you prefer the bumpy cast-on edge next to smooth stitch patterns, that's fine. It's your choice.

Once knitters make the decision, they usually use the same side of the cast-on edge on the public side of all garment pieces for a consistent look. But there are always exceptions. If you are making an asymmetrical garment with one sleeve that is all seed stitch and one sleeve that is all ribbing, you may choose to have the bumpy cast-on edge on the public side of the seed stitch sleeve and the smooth cast-on edge on the public side of the ribbed sleeve.

What you want to avoid is having a sweater—a pullover, for example—that has the smooth cast-on edge on the public side on the back, the bumpy cast-on edge on the public side on the front, and the same stitch pattern above the cast-on edges on both pieces.

When those pieces are seamed together, the different edges will be noticeable.

Right Sides and Wrong Sides

Beginning knitters are often confused by sweater instructions that say: "CO 88 sts and work in K1 P1 Rib until piece measures one inch, ending after a wrong-side row." What's a wrong-side row? K1 P1 ribbing (also called 1×1 ribbing) looks the same on both sides, especially if there aren't any extra stitches added for seaming.

Look at the cast-on edge. Decide which side of the cast on you want on the right side and which side of the cast on you want on the wrong side. Then you'll know which side of the ribbing is the right side and which is the wrong side.

Project Sweater

The pattern for the Baby Cardi, beginning on page 79, offers an opportunity to practice all "seven things" covered in this book. The pattern is divided into sections that correspond with material in each chapter. If you knit the sweater as you read the book, you will be able to practice the lessons of each chapter on a real, but small, sweater. I think of it as a tutorial project, where you get to put the theory into practice right away. At the end of every chapter, in the section called Project Sweater, you will find out which part of the Baby Cardi includes the material just covered. I recommend that you read each chapter first, then work the corresponding part of the sweater. For this chapter, complete *Part 1* of the Baby Cardi on page 80.

Some Right-Side–Wrong-Side Tips

Many stitch patterns have an obvious right side and wrong side, and you need to think about that when you work the first row.

If the bumpy side of the cast on is facing you when you are ready to work the first row:

- Work the first row as a right-side row to place the bumpy side on the right side or public side of the sweater. (If you are working stockinette stitch, knit.)

- Work the first row as a wrong-side row to place the bumpy side on the wrong side or inside of the sweater. (If you are working stockinette stitch, purl.)

If the smooth side of the cast on is facing you when you are ready to work the first row:

- Work the first row as a right-side row to place the smooth side on the right side or public side of the sweater. (If you are working stockinette stitch, knit.)

- Work the first row as a wrong-side row to place the smooth side on the wrong side or inside of the sweater. (If you are working stockinette stitch, purl.)

Overall, the most important thing for you to know is that you have a choice. It is completely your decision, so be sure to make that decision.

Smooth side of cast-on edge on the right side of stockinette stitch.

Smooth side of cast-on edge on the wrong side of stockinette stitch.

Bumpy side of cast-on edge on the right side of stockinette stitch.

Bumpy side of cast-on edge on the wrong side of stockinette stitch.

Chapter 2

Increasing in Ribbing

At the bottom of a sweater piece, we often make a transition from ribbing to stockinette stitch or another stitch pattern. The instructions, "Increase 8 stitches evenly across last rib row" are familiar to most of us. But what is a good method for spacing increases evenly? And which increase technique works well in ribbing? The following methods make the transition from ribbing to another stitch pattern smooth and invisible.

Evenly Spaced Increases—The Concept

Our overall goal is to have approximately the same number of stitches between the increases. We don't need to have exactly the same number of stitches between increases. This is quite a relief to many knitters. Whew! This lack of precision may bother some knitters, but a few stitches more or less between increases won't be visible in the area across the bottom of the sweater.

An important consideration is the placement of the first and last increases on a row. It's good to avoid increasing in the first and last stitches in the row if possible, because the edge stitches become part of the seam allowance. Moving the increases in from the edges by at least one stitch will make the seaming easy.

Knitters use a number of different methods to calculate the spacing of the increases. I prefer the following method, which is simple, straightforward, and avoids working into the first and last stitches on the row. The examples that follow are swatch size (not sweater size) so the numbers are small and easy to work. The same method works for sweaters, too. For the first two examples, we'll ignore the issue of increasing in ribbing and assume we're increasing in stockinette stitch.

Example 1—Evenly Spaced Increases in Stockinette Stitch

The sample has 24 stitches in stockinette stitch. Let's increase 5 stitches evenly on the next knit row.

Step 1: Add 1 to the number of increases.

5 increases + 1 = 6. This is the number of "areas" or "spaces" between increases. There are 6 spaces between the increases. We are trying to determine the number of stitches in each of these spaces. This diagram shows the bottom of the 24-stitch sample with 5 increases (I) and 6 spaces between the increases.

space I space I space I space I space I space

Step 2: Divide the number of stitches in the sample by the number of spaces to determine the number of stitches in each space.

24 sts ÷ 6 spaces = 4 sts per space. There should be 4 stitches in each space between the increases.

Step 3: On the increase row: *K4, inc 1 st; rep from * 4 times, end k4. This diagram shows the bottom of the 24-stitch sample with 4 stitches between each increase.

In a perfect world, the numbers always divide evenly. But in the real world, the numbers rarely divide evenly, right? That's part of why we're having this discussion.

If the numbers don't divide evenly, distribute the extra stitches to some of the spaces. The extra stitches can be added to the spaces at the beginning and end of the row, placed in the center spaces, or distributed alternately to the spaces. Try to distribute them in a balanced manner. You don't want all of them added to spaces on the right side and none of them added to the spaces on the left side.

4sts I 4sts I 4sts I 4sts I 4sts I 4sts

Example 2—Evenly Spaced Increases in Stockinette Stitch (with Leftover Stitches)

The sample has 26 stitches in stockinette stitch. Let's increase 5 stitches evenly on the next knit row.

Step 1: Add 1 to the number of increases.

5 increases + 1 = 6 spaces between increases. This diagram shows the bottom of the 26-stitch sample with 5 increases (I) and 6 spaces between the increases. (This looks the same as Step 1 in Example 1.)

space I space I space I space I space I space

Step 2: Divide the number of stitches in the sample by the number of spaces. If you use a calculator, 26 sts ÷ 6 spaces = 4.333 sts per space. Because we can deal only with whole stitches, not .333 stitches, we have to think of this as 4 sts

Two stitches
left over

4sts I 4sts I 4sts I 4sts I 4sts I 4sts

per space with 2 extra sts. There are 4 stitches in each space, and there are 2 leftover stitches that must be distributed to 2 of the spaces.

Step 3: I decided to add the extra stitches to the spaces at the ends. On the increase row: K5, inc 1 st; *k4, inc 1 st, rep from * 3 times, end k5.

5sts I 4sts I 4sts I 4sts I 4sts I 5sts

Converting Fractions of Stitches to Whole Stitches

If you use a calculator to divide the stitches into the spaces, the answer might come out in fractions of stitches. This happened in an example in this chapter: 26 sts ÷ 6 spaces = 4.333 sts per space. This result means that, to be perfectly even, each of the 6 spaces has 4 full stitches, and each of the 6 spaces also has .333 stitches. We need to convert those fractions of stitches into whole stitches. The calculation is: 6 spaces × .333 stitches per space = 2 full stitches. These are the leftover stitches that now need to be added back to 2 of the spaces.

How to Hide Increases in Ribbing

In ribbing, the bar increase is barely visible when it is placed properly. Remember the bar increase? It's the first increase that many of us learned to work when we were kids. We called it by another name—"knit into the front and the back of a stitch."

To work this increase:

Knit into the front loop of the knit stitch, but do not slip it off the left-hand needle.

Then, knit into the back loop of the same stitch and slip it off the left-hand needle.

When many of us first learned the bar increase, we didn't realize that it is a decorative increase. When this increase is worked into a knit stitch, a horizontal bar or bump directly follows the knit stitch. On the right side of stockinette stitch, this bump is quite noticeable. The bar increase should be used in stockinette stitch only when you want a visible, decorative bump.

In ribbing, however, the bar increase can be almost invisible. When the bar increase is worked into a knit stitch that is followed directly by a purl stitch, the bump will be hidden in the purl area or channel of the ribbing. How versatile! This increase, which is highly visible in stockinette stitch, becomes invisible when properly placed in ribbing.

Now let's space the bar increases evenly and hide them in the ribbing at the same time.

To work the bar increase in ribbing, use the method described earlier to determine the placement of the increases. Then, adjust the placement so that each increase is worked into a knit stitch that is followed directly by a purl stitch. Here's how:

Bar increase worked in stockinette stitch. The bars are to the left of the stitches that were knit into the front and the back.

Example 3—Evenly Spaced Increases in 1×1 Ribbing

The sample has 18 stitches in K1 P1 rib (also called 1×1 rib). Let's increase 4 stitches evenly on the last rib row.

(Assume the 1×1 rib pattern is knit as follows: *K1, p1; rep from * across row. In other words, no adjustments have been made to the pattern edge stitches for sewing seams.)

Step 1: Add 1 to the number of increases.

4 increases + 1 = 5 spaces.

Step 2: Divide the number of stitches in the ribbing by the number of spaces.

18 sts ÷ 5 spaces = 3 sts per space, with 3 extra sts.

Step 3: There will be 2 spaces with 3 sts and 3 spaces with 4 sts.

Step 4: Now look at the stitches on the increase row. These are the stitches on the left-hand needle that you will work across for the last rib row. Place open-ring stitch markers to the left of the knit stitches where the bar increase will be worked. Make adjustments to be sure each bar increase is worked into a knit stitch. Also, be sure that one increase is worked into the last stitch of each space, except for the last space.

Stitches on the left-hand needle just before working the increase row. Notice the first and last spaces have 3 sts. All other spaces have 4 sts.

If you want to double check, count to be sure you have approximately the same number of stitches between markers. Some knitters prefer to hold up the piece and eyeball it to see if the markers look evenly distributed. That works, too. If the markers aren't placed fairly evenly, move them around until the increases look balanced.

Step 5: Work the bar increase into the stitch before each marker. Begin working stockinette stitch on the next row.

Bar increase worked in 1×1 ribbing. The first row of stockinette stitch is a purl row.

To help you see how the increase row is worked, here are written instructions: K1, p1, k into the front and the back of the next stitch, *p1, k1, p1, k into the front and the back of the next stitch; rep from * 2 times, end p1, k1, p1. Instructions like these are usually not included in patterns, so you have to figure it out yourself.

For a K2 P2 rib (also called a 2×2 rib), the calculation is similar. Just remember that the increase should be worked into a knit stitch that is followed directly by a purl stitch so the bump falls into the purl channel. If it is worked into a knit stitch that is followed by a knit stitch, the bump will show up between the two knit stitches.

Example 4—Evenly Spaced Increases in 2×2 Ribbing

The sample has 18 stitches in K2 P2 rib. Let's increase 3 stitches evenly on the last rib row.

(Assume the 2×2 rib pattern is knit as follows: RS rows: *K2, p2; rep from * 3 times, end k2. WS rows: *P2, k2; rep from * 3 times, end p2.)

Step 1: Add 1 to the number of increases.

3 increases + 1 = 4 spaces.

Step 2: Divide the number of stitches in the ribbing by the number of spaces.

18 sts ÷ 4 spaces = 4 sts per space, with 2 extra sts.

Step 3: We expect to have 2 spaces with 4 sts and 2 spaces with 5 sts.

Step 4: Assume the increases are made on a right-side row of ribbing. Look at the stitches on the increase row. These are the stitches on the left-hand needle that you will work across for the last rib row. Make adjustments to be sure each bar increase is worked into a knit stitch that is followed directly by a purl stitch. Place markers.

As we look at the rib row, we see that we can't work the bar increase in the 4th stitch, which is a purl stitch, and we can't work it in the 5th stitch, which is a knit followed by a knit. So the first bar increase is worked into the 6th stitch. Place a marker after the 6th stitch on the row.

Continue counting and placing markers across the row. You will see there is one space with 6 sts and 3 spaces with 4 sts. We did not end up with the spacing we expected, which is OK. If you are bothered by the 6-stitch space being larger than all the others, keep in mind that this is an 18-stitch swatch. Across the bottom of a 74-stitch sweater back or front, one larger space will not be noticeable, and it may not bother you as much.

Bar increase worked in 2×2 ribbing. The first row of stockinette stitch is a purl row.

Bar increase worked in 1×1 ribbing. The first row of stockinette stitch is a knit row.

Bar increase worked in 2×2 ribbing. The first row of stockinette stitch is a knit row.

Step 5: Work the bar increase into the stitch before each marker. Begin working stockinette stitch on the next row.

To help you see how the increase row is worked, here are written instructions: K2, p2, k1, k into the front and the back of the next stitch, *p2, k1, k into the front and the back of the next stitch; rep from * 1 time, end p2, k2.

The bar increase can be worked on either a right-side row or a wrong-side row of ribbing. That means that if the stitch pattern above the ribbing is stockinette stitch, the first row can be either a knit row or a purl row. Whether worked on the right side or the wrong side, the bar increase blends into the rib pattern and is not noticeable.

Project Sweater

Work *Part 2* of the Baby Cardi, on page 80, to increase in ribbing.

"Seven Things" Baby Cardi (pattern on page 79).

Chapter 3

Slanting Decreases

Knit garments are made to fit bodies and accommodate arms and necks. The fabric is shaped by working decreases in certain areas of the garment. Because our bodies are symmetrical, the shaping is done on the right and left sides of the sweater pieces. On the front of a pullover, for example, decreases are worked for the right and left armholes as well as the right and left sides of the neck. There may even be some decreases from the hip to the waist, and then increases from the waist to the bust. This chapter will focus on shaping with decreases. Increases are covered in the next chapter.

When decreases are used in pairs in garments, it looks best if the decreases on the left side of the garment slant in one direction and the decreases on the right side slant in the opposite direction.

Decreases Worked on the Knit Side of Stockinette Stitch

On the knit side of stockinette stitch, k2tog (knit two stitches together) and ssk (slip, slip, knit) look good when used together in garment shaping. K2tog slants to the right and ssk slants to the left. These single-stitch decreases have the same structure and do not have any twisted stitches. They are often referred to as paired, slanting decreases that mirror each other. Both decreases are worked with the knit side of the fabric facing the knitter.

K2TOG (Slants to the Right)

With the right side (knit side) facing you, insert right needle into two stitches on left needle and knit them together.

In this sample, to help you see what is happening in the k2tog, the right stitch is white and the left stitch is violet. Notice how the white, right stitch (which was the first stitch on the left needle) tucks behind the violet, left stitch (which was the second stitch on the left needle). The left stitch comes to the front and creates the overall right slant of the decrease.

SSK (Slants to the Left)

With the right side (knit side) facing you, slip the first stitch knitwise from the left needle to the right needle.

Slip the next stitch knitwise from the left needle to the right needle.

Insert the left needle into the fronts of these two stitches, from left to right, and knit them together.

In this sample, to help you see what is happening in the ssk, the left stitch is white and right stitch is violet. Notice how the white, left stitch (which was the second stitch on the left needle) tucks behind the violet, right stitch (which was the first stitch on the left needle). The right stitch comes to the front of the fabric and creates the overall left slant of the decrease. Because the stitches are slipped knitwise, they aren't twisted when they are knit together.

When the ssk is worked, the slipping usually stretches and elongates the stitches. When this happens, the ssk doesn't look like the mirror image of the k2tog because the front stitch on the ssk looks bigger than the front stitch on the k2tog. The ssk will look neater if you keep the stitches on the tips of the needles as you slip them and try to avoid pulling and stretching them. I find that working on the tips of the needles really helps.

Some knitters have come up with other methods to avoid the elongated stitch. One method is to slip the first stitch knitwise as usual, but then slip the second stitch purlwise. This twists the second stitch and takes up some of the slack of the first stitch. The twisted stitch isn't visible because it is covered by the untwisted stitch on the front. The tighter front stitch makes the ssk look more like the k2tog, but now the structure of the ssk, which has one twisted stitch, does not match the structure of the k2tog.

I prefer the paired slanting decreases that mirror each other in appearance and in structure—with no twisted stitches. I work my ssk by slipping both stitches knitwise on the tips of the needles. Many knitters would consider this the "right way," and if you are submitting your work for evaluation by a jury or for a knitting credential, such as the TKGA Master Hand Knitter, this may be the required method. But in your own sweaters, you have a choice. Just be aware of the differences, and be sure you are happy with the appearance of the paired decreases.

Twisted Stitches: What Are They?

These two swatches and pieces of yarn illustrate the difference between untwisted and twisted stitches.

You want to know and see the difference between twisted and untwisted stiches so you don't twist stitches accidentally. Twisted stitches are not "bad." In fact, they appear in certain stitch patterns and techniques. But know what they are so you can avoid creating them when they are not needed or wanted.

Look closely at the white stitch. It is not twisted. The legs of the stitch do not cross at the bottom. The white piece of yarn to the right of the stitch is put there to show the path of the yarn in the white stitch.

This white stitch is twisted. The legs of the stitch are crossed at the bottom. The white yarn to the right of the stitch shows the path of the yarn in the twisted white stitch. See how the yarn crosses at the bottom.

Decreases Worked on the Purl Side of Stockinette Stitch

It's good to know the wrong-side decreases so you can use them when needed. For example, when shaping a shallow neckline, the decreases are often worked on every row, which means decreases must be worked on both right-side and wrong-side rows.

The p2tog (purl two stitches together) and ssp (slip, slip, purl) are single-stitch decreases, worked on the wrong side, that have the same structure and right-side appearance as the k2tog and ssk. They do not have any twisted stitches.

P2tog, worked on the purl side of stockinette stitch, slants right on the knit side of stockinette stitch. Ssp, worked on the purl side of stockinette stitch, slants left on the knit side of stockinette stitch. It is important to think about how these decreases will look on the knit side, the side opposite from where you'll be working them.

P2TOG (Slants to the Right on the Knit Side of Stockinette Stitch)

With the wrong side (purl side) facing you, insert right needle into two stitches on left needle and purl them together.

On the knit side the p2tog looks the same as the k2tog.

SSP (Slants to the Left on the Knit Side of Stockinette Stitch)

With the wrong side (purl side) facing you, slip the first stitch knitwise from the left needle to the right needle.

Slip the next stitch knitwise from the left needle to the right needle.

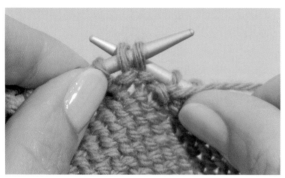

Return these two stitches to the left needle, slipping them back purlwise.

Purl the two stitches together through the back loops (p2tog tbl) as follows:

Turn the tip of the left-hand needle toward you, so you can see the back of the needle. Take the right-hand needle and place it, from the back, through the second stitch from the tip of the left needle, then through the stitch nearest the tip of the left needle.

Bring the right needle to the front, keeping the two stitches on it, and p2tog.

Be sure to slip the stitches knitwise; otherwise you will get twisted stitches. On the knit side, this decrease looks the same as the ssk. The only tricky part is the p2tog tbl.

Placement of Slanting Decreases in Garments

When working decreases in a stockinette stitch sweater, it's best to work them at least one stitch from the edge. If

Know Your Decreases

I strongly recommend that you memorize the slant of the four decreases. Even though you can always look up this information in knitting books, knitters often don't want to take the time to look something up, and you may be knitting on a bus or at a beach or somewhere else where you don't have knitting reference sources at hand.

If you know and understand the slants of the decreases, you can decide which is the appropriate one to use as you are knitting. If a sweater pattern, or even a stitch pattern, tells you to use the ssk, you will be able to decide whether in that particular place a decrease that slants left looks better than one that slants right. If you decide it doesn't, use the k2tog decrease instead.

Also, this knowledge will allow you to decide which way you want the decrease to slant, and then you can use the appropriate decrease technique. You may decide that a right-slanting decrease will look best in a particular place on a right-side row, so you'll use the k2tog.

I urge you to think about the slant of the decrease and how it will look in a particular area of the sweater, rather than think, "I always use the ssk at the beginning of the row, and I always use the k2tog at the end of the row." This may not always be what you do. Full-fashioned shaping techniques provide options for slanting the decreases. Read about these options in the section, Placement of Slanting Decreases in Garments.

you remember to do this, the decrease will not interfere with the edge stitch, and it will be easy to sew the seam. Decreases worked into the second and third stitches on the row and into the third-to-the-last and second-to-the-last stitches on the row will be visible next to the seam (or the edging) on the public side of the finished sweater. These decreases are attractive, but they do not stand out like the full-fashioned decreases, which we'll talk about next.

Full-fashioned Shaping

Full-fashioned shaping, also called full fashion or full fashioning, is a visible line of shaping, either decreasing or increasing, that is used as a design detail in stockinette stitch sweaters. If you look at ready-to-wear sweaters in the stores, you often see a visible line of decreases around armholes and necklines. To use full-fashioned shaping in a handknit stockinette stitch sweater, work the decreases (or increases) two or three stitches from the edge. For example, when you shape armholes on the front of a pullover on a right-side row, work as follows: K3, work decrease, knit to last 5 sts, work decrease, k3.

You have two options for full-fashioned shaping. Remember that in both of these, the decreases are worked in stockinette stitch and they are moved in two or three stitches from the edge.

Option 1—Smooth Line of Shaping
Decreases slant in the same direction as the slant of the edge. In other words, when the armhole or neckline slants left, use a left-slanting decrease. When the armhole or neckline slants right, use a right-slanting decrease. This creates a smooth line of shaping.

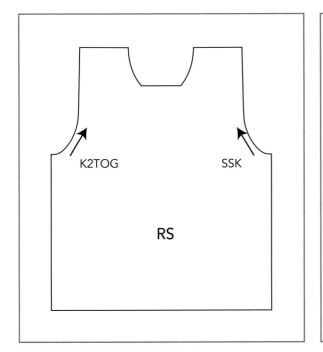
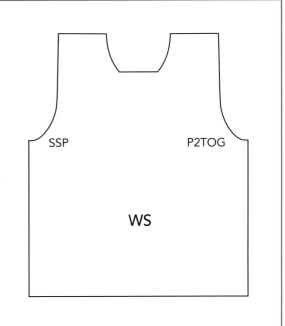

On the right side (RS) of the fabric, work the k2tog and ssk slanting in the same direction as the edge.

On the wrong side (WS) of the fabric, work the p2tog and ssp as shown, so their appearance on the right side looks the same as the k2tog and ssk—slanting in the same direction as the edge.

Tip: When the decreases are worked one stitch from the edge, as discussed at the beginning of this section, it looks nice to slant them in the same direction as the edge, as shown here with full-fashioned shaping.

Option 2—Textured Line of Shaping

Decreases slant against the direction of the slant of the edge. You could also think of these decreases as slanting toward the edges. When the knit piece slants left, use a right-slanting decrease. When the knit piece slants right, use a left-slanting decrease. This creates a textured line of shaping.

On the right side (RS) of the fabric, work the ssk and k2tog slanting against the edge.

On the wrong side (WS) of the fabric, work the p2tog and ssp as shown, so their appearance on the right side looks the same as the k2tog and ssk—slanting against the edge.

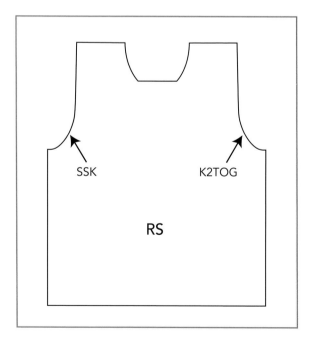

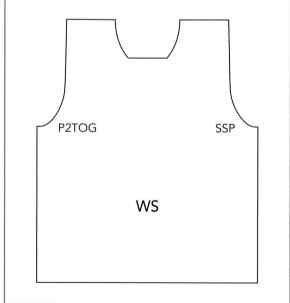

With busy stitch patterns or colorwork designs, a visible line of shaping might interrupt the pattern and interfere with the design. In these cases, work the decreases into the edge stitches so the decreases are invisible. The edge stitches are the first and second stitches in the row and the next-to-the-last and last stitches in the row. Be sure the decreases slant in the same direction as the slant of the edge (as in full-fashioned shaping Option 1). If they don't, it will be difficult to sew an invisible seam.

But, you will ask, didn't you tell us to work the decreases at least one stitch from the edge? Yes, do this in stockinette stitch and the seaming will be easy and straightforward using the basic vertical seaming technique called mattress stitch (see Techniques near the end of the book).

But with fancy stitch patterns and colorwork patterns, work properly slanting decreases on the edge stitches. The technique for seaming these edges—a variation of the invisible horizontal seam—is not necessarily harder, just different. It is possible to sew a very nice, invisible seam on these edges, and the garment will look much nicer because the colorwork or the stitch pattern isn't interrupted.

How to Decrease When Transitioning from One Stitch Pattern to Another

In Chapter 2, you learned how to increase in the last row of ribbing. Sometimes the sweater's bottom edging—ribbing or some other pattern—has more stitches than the body of the sweater, and you need to decrease stitches in the last row of the edging.

When I need to decrease across a row in order to transition from one stitch pattern to another, I like to use the k2tog because it is neat and easy to work. You could use the ssk, but in the following discussion, k2tog is used.

To decrease stitches in the last row of a stitch pattern, determine the placement of the decreases in the same way you calculated the increase placement in Chapter 2. Then look at the stitches, keeping in mind the structure of the k2tog decrease (left stitch moves to the front, right stitch goes to the back). To determine the placement of the decreases, look at the two stitches that will be knit together. If the decrease looks good when the right stitch tucks behind the left stitch, place it there. If not, move it by a stitch or two. Again, try to space the decreases at approximately equal intervals, but the intervals don't have to be exactly the same number of stitches.

Example—Evenly Spaced Decreases in 1×1 Ribbing

The sample has 20 stitches in 1×1 rib. Let's decrease 4 stitches evenly across the last rib row.

Step 1: Add 1 to the number of decreases.

4 stitches + 1 = 5 spaces between decreases.

Step 2: Divide the number of sts in the ribbing by the number of spaces.

20 stitches ÷ 5 spaces = 4 sts per space.

Place a stitch marker after every 4th stitch. Now examine the stitches. At each marker, a purl stitch is before the marker and a knit stitch is after the marker. If you knit these two stitches together, the knit stitch will come to the front and cover the purl stitch, which will look good.

Move each marker one stitch to the left. When working across the row in pattern, knit together the two stitches immediately before the marker. Work all other stitches in pattern.

To help you see how the decrease row is worked, here are written instructions: K1, p1, k1, k2tog, *p1, k1, k2tog; rep from * 2 times, end p1, k1, p1.

Project Sweater

Work *Part 3* of the Baby Cardi, on page 80, to work paired, slanting decreases. Part 3 includes both the left front and the right front, so you will be working the Chapter 1 and 2 techniques again.

Chapter 4
Invisible Increases

Increases, like decreases, are often worked in pairs to shape garment pieces. Increases shape sleeves from the wrist to the underarm, and body pieces from the waist to the bust. When increases are used in pairs, they look best if they mirror each other.

The Make One Increase

The make one increase (M1) is barely visible and can be used in many places. It is made by working into the horizontal strand of yarn between two stitches. This strand is called a running thread. The increase can be worked on the right side or the wrong side in stockinette stitch and in other stitch patterns. The running thread can be knit or purled, so the new stitch can be easily worked into a stitch pattern. There is a right-slanting M1 and a left-slanting M1, and they can be used together for mirrored shaping of symmetrical garment pieces.

Increases Worked on the Knit Side of Stockinette Stitch

M1 Right (Slants to the Right)

With the right side (knit side) facing you, place the left needle from back to front under the horizontal strand between the stitch just worked on the right needle and the first stitch on the left needle.

Use your left index finger to create some slack in the running thread on the left needle. The running thread is usually tight and it's hard to get the right needle into it.

Knit the strand through the front loop. This twists the strand and prevents a hole.

M1 Left (Slants to the Left)

With the right side (knit side) facing you, place the left needle from front to back under the horizontal strand between the stitch just worked on the right needle and the first stitch on the left needle.

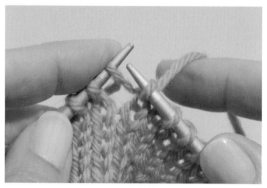

Again, use your left index finger to create some slack in the running thread.

Knit the strand through the back loop by placing the right needle through the far side of the strand on the left needle. This twists the strand and prevents a hole.

Many knitters like to use the right needle as a tool to scoop up the running thread and place it on the left needle. It's all right to do this. What's important is how the left needle picks up the running thread. It is either front to back or back to front.

Why Is There a Hole?

If you don't twist the horizontal strand when you work an M1 increase, you will become acquainted with another version of the M1— the decorative M1. When the running thread is not twisted, a large hole appears in the fabric. This hole can be an intentional, decorative element in a stitch pattern or in a shaped area of a sweater, and in that situation it looks fine. But when we don't want that hole and we get it by mistake, I jokingly call it the "big-gaping-hole make one."

Even when the twisted versions of the M1 increase are worked correctly, sometimes small holes appear. This is usually caused by tight stitch tension, so try working the M1 stitch a little looser and see if that fixes the problem. Keep in mind that holes are often caused by working too loosely, but also sometimes by working too tightly and pulling the yarn together, which can create open spaces or gaps. If working looser doesn't get rid of small holes, then try working a little tighter.

The white stitches in this sample were knit into the running thread. Examine the M1 Right (the increase on the right): Below the white stitch, the right side of the twisted running thread is prominent and creates the right slant of the increase. Now look at the M1 Left (the increase on the left): Below the white stitch, the left side of the twisted running thread is prominent and creates the left slant of the increase.

Increases Worked on the Purl Side of Stockinette Stitch

Increases, like the sleeve increases from the wrist to the underarm, are usually worked on right-side rows. But it's good to know the wrong-side increases because there are always exceptions to the right-side tradition. My students tell me about them all the time, in fact.

When increases are worked on the wrong side, what matters is how they look on the right side of the fabric, the side where the slant is visible.

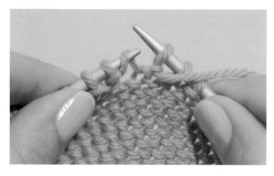

Wrong Side M1—Version 1 (Slants to the Right on the Knit Side of Stockinette Stitch)

With the wrong side (purl side) facing you, place the left needle from back to front under the horizontal strand between the stitch just worked on the right needle and the first stitch on the left needle.

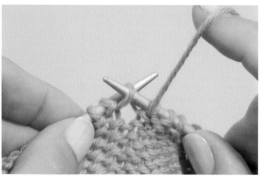

Purl the strand through the front loop. This twists the strand and prevents a hole.

Wrong Side M1—Version 2 (Slants to the Left on the Knit Side of Stockinette Stitch)

With the wrong side (purl side) facing you, place the left needle from front to back under the horizontal strand between the stitch just worked on the right needle and the first stitch on the left needle.

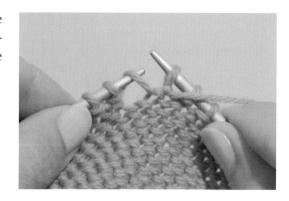

Purl the strand through the back loop. To do this, turn the tip of the left-hand needle toward you, so you can see the back of the needle, and place the right-hand needle, from the back, through the stitch. As you do this, both tips will be pointing in the same direction. Bring the right needle to the front and purl. Purling through the back loop twists the strand and prevents a hole.

As with the M1 increases worked on the right side, you can pick up the running thread with your right needle and place it on the left needle. Also, use your left index finger to help create slack in the running thread. If you see a hole after working the M1, review "Why Is There a Hole?" on page 37.

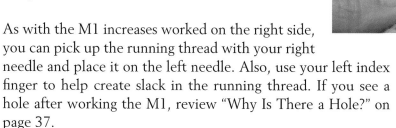

Placement of Slanting Increases in Garments

Because the M1 increases are worked between two stitches, they will always be at least one stitch away from the edge. When shaping garments, it looks nice to use the M1 Right at the edge that slants to the right and the M1 Left at the edge that slants to the left. For example, when knitting a sleeve from the wrist to the underarm, work the increases as follows on the RS: K1, M1 Right, knit across until 1 st remains, M1 Left, k1.

M1 increases can also be used with full-fashioned shaping, the visible line of shaping discussed in Chapter 3. Just as with the decreases described in Chapter 3, move the increases 2 or 3 stitches in from the edges, and either slant both increases with the edge or slant both increases against the edge.

In other words, for a stockinette stitch sleeve worked from the wrist to the underarm:

- The increases will slant with the edge when worked on the right side as follows: K3, M1 Right, knit across until 3 sts remain, M1 Left, k3; or

- The increases will slant against the edge when worked on the right side as follows: K3, M1 Left, knit across until 3 sts remain, M1 Right, k3.

You want to know and remember the increase techniques and placement options because increases, like decreases, are used in sweater shaping.

Project Sweater

Work *Part 4* of the Baby Cardi, on page 81, to work paired, slanting increases. Skills covered in Chapters 1–4 will be practiced again, also.

Two-Texture Pullover (pattern on page 97).

Chapter 5

Blocking

Blocking helps to even out the stitches in a knit fabric. It makes the edges of the fabric straight and flat, but appropriate blocking does not crush the fabric or stitch patterns. Most stitch patterns, including stockinette stitch, look better after being blocked. Care should be taken with textured stitch patterns, like bobbles and cables, so they are not smashed or crushed.

There are various ways to block sweaters or sweater pieces. If we asked a panel of expert knitters, each member of the panel would probably recommend a slightly different method. That's why it's important for you to figure out what works for you. But be sure to block your knitting—it will look better.

I always block my sweater pieces before I sew them together. Edges of knit fabric tend to roll, which makes them hard to seam. Blocking makes the edges flat and smooth and thus easier to seam. Also, it's easier to work with each piece separately, rather than the entire sweater, for the first blocking.

Wet Blocking

Spread out towels and lay the sweater pieces on the towels. Don't overlap the pieces. Then spray each piece with a plant sprayer bottle full of room temperature water. Spray each piece until it is completely soaking wet. An alternative method would be to wet each piece thoroughly and then lay it out on the towels. Measure each piece to be sure it is the right size. Don't stretch ribbing or other elastic stitches. Pinning often isn't necessary because the weight of the wet fabric helps to flatten the edges and keep them from curling. If you must pin, be careful about using metal pins because they can rust. Rust marks will not be easy to remove from the knit fabric.

After you measure the pieces to make sure they're sized correctly, do what I call the "patting motion," which is to touch the surface of the fabric and make sure it's smooth. This is not a smashing or pressing motion. It is similar to what you do after washing a sweater, when you lay it out and pat it into shape to dry. If you think about it, every time you wash a sweater, you block it again. That's what is happening here, only you're working with the separate pieces.

Leave the sweater pieces on the towels overnight, then remove the towels the next day and allow the pieces to lie flat and dry thoroughly. Sweater-drying racks (wood or plastic frames covered with a mesh fabric) are great for this final stage because the air can circulate under the pieces as they dry. In my house, we call these racks "cat hammocks" because our cats love to sleep on them when no one is looking.

Blocking a Baby Cardi sleeve.

Steam Blocking

Steam blocking makes use of the hot spray from a steam iron. Lay out the sweater pieces on a towel or ironing board, face down. Hold the iron several inches from the surface of the fabric and allow the steam to spray down onto the wrong side or inside of the fabric. Don't let the iron touch or rest on the hand-knit fabric because it can scorch it or smash the texture. You aren't pressing here, just misting.

An alternative method is to lay out the pieces with the right side facing up and place a clean cloth, or blocking cloth, over the fabric to protect it from the hot steam. As the fabric cools a little, use your hand to do the patting motion and measure to be sure the pieces are the correct size. Again, be careful about pinning because the steam can rust some types of metal pins.

Keep the pieces flat until they start to feel dry; then put them on a sweater-drying rack or a flat surface until they are completely dry. The drying time will be faster than with wet blocking.

Be cautious when you steam block: after a piece is blocked, you may not be able to change it. In other words, once the fabric is overblocked (and by that I mean smashed, flattened, stretched, or with the elasticity removed), it cannot return to its previous state. Therefore, ribbing and other elastic fabrics should not be blocked with steam. If you are using steam, just avoid those sections of the sweater. Also, certain yarns should not be steam blocked. Acrylic yarns and novelty yarns can melt from the heat of the steam. Hairy fibers, like mohair and angora, may become matted.

Blocking Seams

Seams usually look better with a little blocking.

After you sew the sweater together, lay the seam areas flat and lightly spray or steam. Allow to dry. For vests, all seams can be blocked at once. For sweaters, you will have to do this in stages because you can't lay all the seams flat at the same time. If the sweater is a cardigan, both side seams can be blocked at the same time, but it's a little trickier with the side seams of a pullover. For any garment, keep in mind that the rest of the sweater has already been blocked, so be careful not to block any new folds or creases in other areas of

the sweater when blocking the seams. In this picture, the blue pins are placed on the vest to show the seams that are being blocked (the pins are not actually needed for this part of the blocking process).

Which Method Should I Use?

Several things will help you determine which method to use: the fibers, the stitch pattern, and the amount of space you can devote to blocking. Start by reading the yarn label, then think about the texture and appearance of the stitch pattern. Determine the amount of space available for spreading out sweater pieces and leaving them to dry for a day or two. Always block your swatch first to see whether you're happy with the method you have chosen.

Fiber

Read the yarn label to remind yourself of the fiber content of the yarn. Because many yarns are made of new and different fibers, it's good to see whether the manufacturer gives any washing instructions or blocking advice on the label. If you can hand wash a yarn, you will be able to wet block it. Some yarns have "Dry Clean Only" on the label, but many of those, too, can be hand washed and wet blocked. Wool can be wet blocked or steam blocked. But remember, some yarns will melt or mat if they are hit with a shot of steam. Consider these differences, then practice on your swatch.

Stitch Pattern

Although many types of knitting can be wet blocked or steamed, some knitting really benefits from steam. Stranded colorwork fabrics sometimes ripple a little, and steam can often flatten the ripples better than wet blocking.

Whichever method you use, be sure textured stitches like cables and bobbles are not crushed. Lace knitting, especially shawls, requires special treatment, so be sure to follow the designer's instructions on blocking or seek out the advice of an experienced lace knitter.

Amount of Space

After considering the fiber content and stitch pattern, you should be able to choose a blocking method. Now you need to consider how much space you have available for blocking and how long you can dedicate that space to blocking. This may influence your final decision. Because steamed pieces dry faster than wet ones, they will occupy the "blocking space" for a shorter amount of time.

If you have a place to lay out all the sweater pieces and leave them for several days, wet blocking will be easy. If the space is available only for a shorter time, steaming may be your choice. If you don't have very much space, you may need to use one small space and block pieces in shifts. In this case, wet blocking will take considerably longer than steaming because each piece should dry thoroughly before it is moved.

With both methods, the pieces need to dry in a place where pets and people won't disturb them. In my experience, cats hate to get wet, but they love to sleep on wet sweaters!

Choose a Method, Then Practice

Pick a method of blocking that works for you and use it. Some of your decision will come down to personal preference. I wet block my sweater pieces because I have more control over the result, with no risk of overblocking. Steam blocking, which I did for many years, isn't necessary for most of my sweaters.

Although I knit with lots of wool and natural fibers, I do incorporate other fibers, which can't be steam blocked, into some of my sweaters. I knit quite a few slip-stitch patterns, entrelac pieces, and free-form designs, which look fine with wet blocking. And I am fortunate to have a big table where I can leave wet things for days. So I always wet block unless the fiber or the stitch pattern tell me I shouldn't.

A final piece of advice on blocking: practice on your swatch, don't practice on your sweater. Uncover all the surprises and problems when you block your swatch, adjust for them, and then you won't have any mishaps with the sweater.

Project Sweater

Work *Part 5* of the Baby Cardi, on page 81. This section includes blocking the sweater pieces and sewing seams (see Techniques).

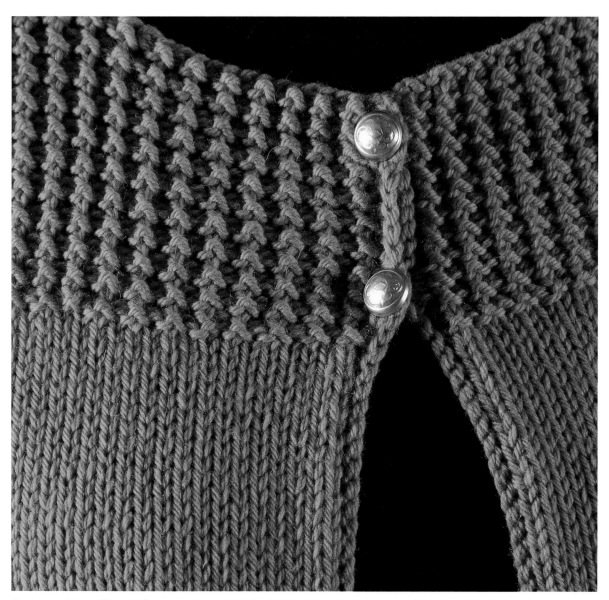

Sweater without Sleeves (pattern on page 101).

Chapter 6

Picking Up Stitches for Bands

Let's talk about bands, also called edgings and borders, that are created after the sweater is sewn together. Stitches for the band are worked directly onto the sweater's edge, then the band is knit from there. The goal is to have a band with the correct number of stitches so that it lies flat and smooth. If the band has too many stitches, it will ripple and flare. If the band doesn't have enough stitches, it will pull in and pucker the sweater. The technique used to create these stitches is called "pick up and knit."

The Technique: Pick Up and Knit

To pick up and knit means to place a knitting needle from front to back through the sweater fabric near the edge, bring the yarn around the needle as if you were knitting a stitch, and pull a loop through the fabric. The loop is now a stitch on the needle. That is the entire technique—pick up and knit. There is nothing more (or less) involved. I will describe the details of this technique in the following paragraphs.

You need to know how to do this technique and you need to know what it is called. Many knitters feel that the term pick up and knit does not accurately describe this technique. It may not literally describe it, but in the language of knitting, this is exactly what it means. This is a standard knitting term used in many patterns, so you want to know, understand, and memorize the meaning, just as you would if you were learning another language.

Use a knitting needle that is two sizes smaller than the needle you used to knit the sweater. Hold the edge of the knit fabric with the right side facing you.

The Technique for Horizontal Edges

Horizontal edges are bound-off edges, like the center of a neckline.

Identify the stitches just inside the bound-off edge. A single stitch looks like the letter V.

Place the right needle into the center of a stitch just inside the bound-off edge. (The pick-up-and-knit technique has already been used to create four stitches on the needle.)

Bring the yarn around the right needle (as you do when knitting a stitch) and pull the loop through the fabric. You have created one stitch that is now on the needle. Repeat until you have the desired number of stitches. (The fifth stitch has just been created on the needle.)

Stitches on the needle after the pick-up-and-knit technique has been worked on a horizontal edge.

After the band is created, the stitches on the band line up vertically with the stitches in the body as shown in this picture.

When picking up and knitting, if you put the right needle under the chain of the bind off, rather than through the center of the stitch just inside the bind off, the band stitches will be off-set by a half stitch from the body stitches and the line of stitches will be interrupted.

The Technique for Vertical Edges

The front edges of a cardigan are an example of vertical edges.

Place the right needle between the first and second stitches at the edge. Carefully examine the edge to find these two stitches (or Vs). The edge stitch, as seen in the photo, usually rolls under a little. Be sure to put the needle completely through the fabric, between the two stitches. (The pick-up-and-knit technique has already been used to create six stitches on the needle.)

Bring the yarn around the right needle and pull the loop through the fabric. You have created one stitch, which is now on the needle. Repeat until you have the desired number of stitches.

Stitches on the needle after the pick-up-and-knit technique has been worked on a vertical edge. A column of whole stitches is next to the needle.

On the sweater body, a column of whole stitches is next to the band (as shown in the top picture).

One whole stitch—the first stitch or edge stitch—turns under and goes to the back of the work, creating a seam allowance on the wrong side (as shown in the bottom picture).

When picking up and knitting on vertical edges, you could work into the center of the edge stitch, so only a half stitch is turned under to the wrong side. Although this half-stitch method produces a less bulky seam allowance, the method that places a whole stitch into the seam allowance has two advantages. First, the attachment of the band to the sweater is more secure if you work between the edge stitch and the next stitch. Second, edge stitches are often loose and loopy. If stitches are picked up and knit in the center of the edge stitches, half of each loose, loopy stitch remains on the public side (outside) of the sweater. It's better to have those loose, loopy edge stitches hidden in the seam allowance so they are not visible on the right side.

While the whole-stitch seam allowance seems to create bulk on the wrong side, the seam allowance is to the scale or gauge of the sweater. In other words, a bulky yarn creates a seam allowance that is appropriate on a sweater made with a bulky yarn. A fingering-weight yarn creates a seam allowance that is appropriate on a sweater made in a lightweight yarn.

After you pick up and knit all the required stitches, change to the needle size specified for the band. It may be the same size used for the pickup, but it may be a larger or smaller size.

How Many Stitches Do I Pick Up and Knit?

Pattern directions usually tell you how many stitches to pick up and knit. But there are also standard guidelines and basic calculations that will help you determine the correct number of stitches for your particular sweater. Let's talk about each of these.

Pattern Directions

The directions for a sweater will tell the knitter to pick up and knit a certain number of stitches for the band. Here's an example of the instructions for the front band on a cardigan: "With RS facing and smaller needle, beg at bottom right front edge and pick up and knit 102 (104, 108, 110) sts evenly along right front edge." Always treat that number as a guideline, not the absolute number of stitches you must pick up and knit.

The real meaning of the instructions is: *"With RS facing and smaller needle, beg at bottom right front edge and pick up and knit evenly along right front edge as many stitches as you need to make the band lie flat and smooth."*

Consider the number of stitches in the pattern to be a guideline, and don't worry if you don't end up with the same number. You may have more rows or fewer rows in your sweater piece than the pattern assumes, and that will give you a different number of stitches for the vertical, front band.

Why would you have more or fewer rows? When you knit a sweater from bottom to top, it is more important to get the specified stitch gauge than the specified row gauge. With the correct stitch gauge, the horizontal measurements of the sweater, like the bust and shoulder, will match those of the sweater size you have chosen. If a certain needle size gives you the stitch gauge you need, but you have more or fewer rows to the inch than specified, it's OK. You will still achieve the correct length for the sweater because patterns often allow for the row gauge discrepancy. At certain places, the pattern will state, "work even until piece measures *x* inches." If you follow those directions, the length of the body, armholes, necklines, and sleeves will be correct.

Standard Guidelines

There are guidelines for the number of stitches to pick up and knit on sweater edges.

On horizontal edges, pick up and knit one stitch in each stitch.

On vertical edges, to keep the band from flaring, the guideline is to pick up and knit 3 stitches in every 4 rows. To do this, work one stitch in from the edge and pick up and knit in the first row, pick up and knit in the second row, pick up and knit in the third row, and then skip the fourth row. Pick up and knit in the fifth, sixth, and seventh rows, then skip the eighth row, and so on. On vertical edges, skipping rows will not create a hole because the band will fill in and cover these spaces.

This guideline for vertical edges is based on a typical ratio of the stitch gauge of the band to the row gauge of the sweater. For example, if the band gauge is 5 stitches per inch and the sweater gauge is 6.75 rows per inch, you need to pick up and knit 5 stitches in 6.75 rows. The ratio is $5 \div 6.75$ or .74. This is close to .75 or three-quarters. So the guideline is to pick up and knit 3 stitches in every 4 rows.

For vertical and horizontal edges, practice picking up and knitting stitches on your sweater gauge swatch to be sure the band is flat.

What If the Guideline Doesn't Work?

If the guideline for a vertical edge or a horizontal edge doesn't work and the band either flares or pulls in, the ratio needs to be changed.

How to Change the Ratio for the Vertical Edge

For a more precise ratio on vertical edges, compare the stitch gauge of the band to the row gauge of the sweater.

First, knit a swatch of the band. Be sure to cast on enough stitches for at least four inches. Casting on for eight inches or more is even better to get an accurate gauge measurement. If you are going to block the band on the sweater, block the swatch of the band. Measure the swatch and calculate the stitch gauge. Because the band will not be stretched when it's on the front of a cardigan, don't stretch the band swatch when you measure it.

How to Swatch Ribbing for Bands

To swatch an elastic stitch pattern—like ribbing—for a sweater band, be sure to knit exactly the same number of rows that will be in the band. Although a longer swatch is usually better than a shorter one, the more rows that ribbing has, the more it will pull in horizontally. So a swatch made of 20 rows of ribbing will have more stitches per inch than a swatch with 5 rows of the same ribbing. This is one case where a swatch with more rows is not better, because it won't give you an accurate gauge measurement for a 5-row band.

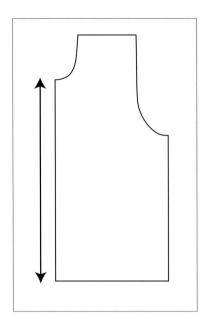

Second, measure the row gauge of the front of your sweater. Again, be sure to measure a significant area, eight inches or more.

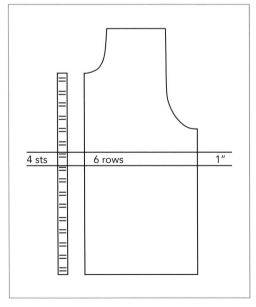

4 sts   6 rows   1"

Then use these numbers to calculate the new ratio.

Example: The band's gauge is 32 stitches to 8 inches, or 4 stitches per inch. The sweater's row gauge is 48 rows to 8 inches, or 6 rows per inch. The ratio is 4 stitches to 6 rows or $^4/_6$. Reduce this fraction to $^2/_3$. Then pick up and knit 2 stitches in every 3 rows. You can see why the ratio 3 out of 4 won't work for this particular sweater.

If you divide the gauges and get a ratio like .7, which is 7 stitches for 10 rows, don't pick up and knit 7 stitches and then skip 3; that would create a hole. Instead, pick up and knit *2 stitches in the next 3 rows, 2 stitches in the next 3 rows, 3 stitches in the next 4 rows; rep from *. (Another way to say this is: *Pick up and knit 2, skip 1, pick up and knit 2, skip 1, pick up and knit 3 skip 1; rep from *) To clarify what is happening, add up the stitches: 2 + 2 + 3 = 7 stitches. Add up the rows 3 + 3 + 4 = 10 rows. This accounts for 7 picked-up stitches for every 10 rows, but it doesn't leave all of the skipped stitches in one place.

The 3 out of 4 guideline ratio for vertical edges sometimes doesn't work. To reduce my frustration, I always start by measuring the gauges and calculating the ratio. I use this new ratio to practice picking up and knitting a band on my swatch. I feel I'm saving time because if I start with the guideline ratio and it doesn't work, I'll have to go through the steps of calculating the correct ratio anyway.

How to Change the Ratio for the Horizontal Edge

The one-to-one guideline ratio for picking up and knitting stitches on a horizontal edge usually works. If the band pulls in or flares when you practice knitting it on the sweater swatch, follow the steps already presented to calculate a new ratio. For horizontal edges, compare the stitch gauge of the band with the stitch gauge of the sweater.

Necklines

Necklines have three types of edges: the horizontal bound-off edge, the straight vertical edge, and the shaped edge that transitions from the horizontal edge to the vertical. Don't wait until the sweater knitting is finished to start thinking about the neckline edging. Be sure to plan for the neckline edging as you knit the sweater and shape the neckline.

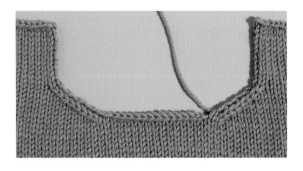

Shaping the Neckline Edge for a Flawless Band Attachment

If possible, move the decreases in at least one stitch from the edge or use full-fashioned shaping, which will move the decreases in several stitches from the edge. The edge stitch will become the seam allowance and will turn under to the wrong side when you pick up and knit the stitches for the band.

If you're using a fancy stitch pattern or a colorwork pattern and the decreases must be worked on the edge, be sure the decreases slant with the direction of the piece to create a smooth line of shaping (see Chapter 3). In other words, use ssk when the neckline slants to the left, and use k2tog when the neckline slants to the right. If the neckline is not shaped with both the ssk and the k2tog slanting in the proper directions, it will be difficult to create an attractive picked-up edge. For example, if the k2tog decrease is worked on the edge stitches on both sides of the neckline, the right-slanting side of the neckline will look smooth at the place where the band and sweater meet, but the left-slanting side may look irregular and bumpy at that place.

Creating the Band Stitches on Shaped Edges

On the curved area of the neckline, measure around the neckline using a flexible ruler or a tape measure standing on its side, or by pivoting a flat ruler. Place plastic safety pins (or some other marker that won't fall out) at one-inch increments. Measure the stitch gauge of the sweater band swatch. Then pick up and knit the appropriate number of stitches, for example, 4 stitches, between the markers. This number is based on the previous example of a band with a gauge of 4 stitches per inch.

Holes on Curved Edges

In the photograph, the tapestry needles are pointing to the transition between the horizontal neckline edge and the shaped neckline edge. Often, the hole is already there in the knitting. Knitters often try to get rid of the hole by picking up a stitch in it. But what always happens? The hole gets bigger.

If you see a hole in the fabric, never pick up and knit a stitch in the hole. The best way to get rid of any hole is to pick up and knit in the stitch just before the hole and pick up and knit in the stitch just after the hole. This helps to close up the hole.

On shaped edges, if you see a hole after you've picked up and knit a stitch, go back and remove the stitch right away. Knitters are optimistic people, so we think that if we knit a few rows, the hole will disappear. But five or six rows later, the hole is usually still there. Shouldn't there be a name for this phenomenon?

Holes often appear on neckline edges at the place where the horizontal edge of the neckline meets the shaped edge.

Center Neckline Stitches

I recommend that you bind off the center, horizontal stitches when you shape a neckline. This will help to stabilize the neckline so it will fit well and keep its shape. Also, because all stitches around the neckline will be picked up and knit, and the transition from sweater to band will look uniform around the whole neckline.

Some patterns suggest placing the center neck stitches on a holder. The neck band is then created by picking up and knitting the stitches on one side of the neckline, knitting the live stitches (the ones put on the holder), then picking up and knitting the stitches along the other side of the neckline. If the neck opening is very small and you need elasticity for it to fit over your head, you may need to do this. It is often done with babies' pullovers too, because the elasticity makes it easy to pull the sweater over the baby's head. But be careful not to stretch the stitches on the holder; sometimes an unattractive row of elongated stitches appears on the finished sweater in the horizontal area where the band and sweater meet.

You usually have a choice, though, so read the pattern carefully to see if there is a reason why you must put the center neck stitches on a holder. If not, I suggest you stabilize the neckline by binding off the stitches.

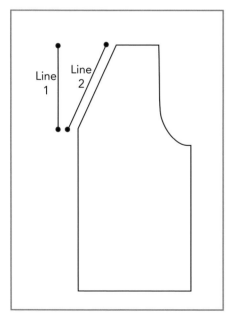

Left front of a V-neck cardigan.

V-Necks

Look at the V-neck cardigan schematic. Let's assume we are using the 3 out of 4 ratio on the vertical section to pick up and knit stitches. On the top section, line 1 shows what the edge would be like if it continued vertically. If the edge were like that, the 3 out of 4 ratio would be used for picking up the stitches. But notice what happens to this line when the neck edge becomes a V-neck. The neckline edge, represented by line 2, is longer than line 1. So line 2 needs more stitches than line 1. But both lines have the same number of rows. Therefore, the 3 out of 4 ratio used on the vertical edge (line 1) will not result in enough stitches on the longer edge (line 2).

The best way to get the correct number of stitches on the V-neck edge is to mark off one-inch increments along that edge. Again, use plastic safety pins or some other kind of marker that won't fall out when the piece is moved. Then pick up and knit the appropriate number of stitches, for example, 4 stitches, between the markers. This number is based on the previous example of a band with a gauge of 4 stitches per inch.

I need to say that all of this is "in theory." Sometimes knitters use the same ratio on the V-neck as on vertical edges, and they don't have any problems with the band. It will depend on the depth and the angle of the V-neck and whether gentle blocking can even out the fabric. But why take chances? You won't find out whether the vertical ratio is successful on your V-neck until you've finished knitting the entire band, and if it isn't, the only option you have is to rip out the band. Measuring the one-inch increments can save time and avoid aggravation.

Practice Is Key

Practice on your swatch, don't practice on your sweater. I say it again and again, because it's important. Picking up stitches for a band can be an anxiety-producing experience. Even with careful calculating and planning, you never really know if it's going to look good until you're finished. That's why, after you've calculated the ratio, it's good to pick up and knit the band on your gauge swatch.

If the band pulls in or flares, take it out, tweak the ratio, and practice again. Keep practicing until you are satisfied that the band will be flat and smooth. You will avoid the wear and tear of practicing on the sweater, and you'll reduce your own frustration over ripping out the sweater band. Or, as I like to say, you'll reduce the wear and tear on your sweater *and* on yourself. When you start picking up and knitting stitches on your sweater, you won't have any anxiety because you know the ratio will work and the band will look great.

Project Sweater

OK, I know I promised that each chapter would have a corresponding part of the Baby Cardi for you to work. But because bands and buttonholes are worked together, and because you need to mark the buttonhole placement (discussed in the next chapter) before you pick up and knit the band stitches, Parts 6 and 7 will be worked together. So take the rest of the day off. Relax. When you are ready, read Chapter 7 and then work *Part 6* and *Part 7* of the Baby Cardi.

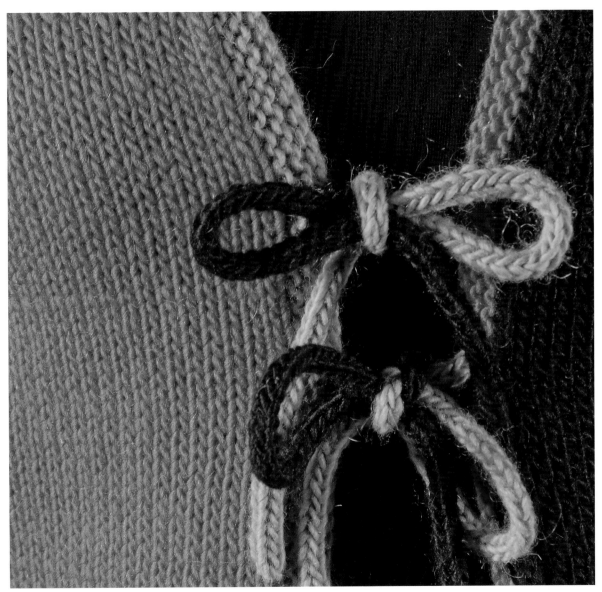

Color Tie Cardigan (pattern on page 107).

Chapter 7

Buttonholes

Cardigans and buttonholes go together. Although you have other choices for closures—like zippers, ties, and frogs—if you knit cardigans, sooner or later you will have to make a buttonhole. The buttonhole described in this chapter looks neat whether buttoned or unbuttoned, fits snugly around the button, and is not difficult to make. But before we go through the buttonhole technique, let's talk about the placement of buttonholes in a garment.

Placement of Buttonholes on the Front Band of a Cardigan

After you sew the sweater together, lay it out flat. Place the buttons on the sweater to determine where they look best. The guideline for button placement is that the top button should be about ½ to 1 inch from the top edge. The bottom button should be ½ to 1 inch from the bottom edge. The actual measurement will depend on the size of the buttons, which could be anywhere from ¼ inch to 3 or more inches in diameter. Top and bottom button placement also depends on the style of the garment—a sweater could have only one or a few buttons at the top and none at the bottom, or it could have only one button in the middle.

Determine the placement of the top and bottom buttons and place markers on the sweater at these points. Measure the distance between these two buttons, and then space the other buttons evenly in between. Be sure to use enough buttons so that the sweater won't pull open between the buttons. It's better to have one too many buttons than not enough.

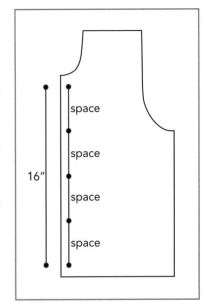

Here's an example: Let's assume the top and bottom button placement is determined and markers are attached. The distance between the top and bottom buttons is 16 inches. Five buttons will be used: the top and bottom buttons and three buttons spaced evenly in between. Thus, there will be four spaces between the buttons.

16 inches ÷ 4 spaces = 4 inches per space.

Place markers at 4-inch intervals between the top and bottom buttons.

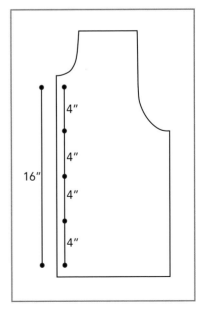

What if the intervals aren't an even number like 4, but are something like 4.188, a measurement that is not easy to find on a ruler? Use the line between the 4-inch mark and the 4$\frac{1}{4}$-inch mark on the ruler and try to make sure each interval is close to the same measurement. Work at it a little until you think the spacing is even. Then stand back and take in the overall view. If everything looks even and balanced to your eye, place the markers for the buttons.

Then, on the other front edge, place corresponding markers for the buttonholes. When you knit the band on that side, work a buttonhole at each marker.

One-row horizontal buttonhole in stockinette stitch.

Buttonhole Technique

This traditional one-row horizontal buttonhole, a popular buttonhole which has several variations, has been used by knitters for many years. It is attractive and can be worked in any stitch pattern. It is firm and self-reinforcing, so you won't have to stitch around it later to tighten it up. It can be worked on the right side or the wrong side of the fabric. This buttonhole can span two or more stitches, so be sure to size it to fit the buttons.

This buttonhole is not difficult to work, but I am showing it in great detail, with lots of pictures, so you can see all the steps. I'm also including some tips to help you as you work it. The cable cast on is used in this buttonhole, and all the steps of the cast on are pictured here. In this buttonhole, slip all stitches **purlwise.**

Work in pattern to the buttonhole. (The sample pictured is worked in 1×1 ribbing.)

Slip the next stitch purlwise from the left needle to the right needle with the yarn in front.

Tip: If the last stitch worked before the buttonhole was a knit stitch (as shown here), bring yarn to front, between the needles, and slip a stitch purlwise. If the last stitch worked before the buttonhole was a purl stitch, the yarn is already in front, so you don't have to move it; in this case, just slip a stitch purlwise.

Take the yarn between the two needles to the back and leave it there.

Slip the next stitch purlwise from the left needle to the right needle.

Use the left needle to pull the first slipped stitch over the second slipped stitch, as you do when you bind off a stitch. Repeat this purlwise slip-and-bind-off maneuver until the desired number of stitches have been bound off. Remember that you are not knitting the stitches, just slipping them purlwise.

Tip: If you are working this buttonhole for the first time, drop the yarn from the hand you use to hold the yarn because you will not be knitting the stitches— only slipping them. If you keep the yarn in your knitting hand, there is a very good chance that you will unknowingly knit with it. After you've made this buttonhole several times, you won't need to drop the yarn from your hand.

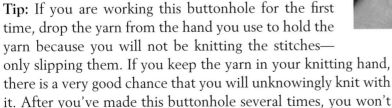

Slip the last bound-off stitch . . .

. . . to the left needle purlwise.

Turn the work. This means take the needle that is in your right hand and put it in your left hand. Take the needle that is in your left hand and put it in your right hand. This is what you usually do at the end of a row—turn the work.

Take the yarn to the back. It will be attached to the work near the left needle. Using the cable cast on with the yarn at the back, cast on as follows:

With yarn in back, insert the right needle between the first and second stitches on the left needle. Bring the yarn around the right needle as if you are knitting a stitch and pull up a loop.

Place the loop on the left needle, twisting it as you place it on the left needle.

Tip: I call this motion "scoop under." The left needle scoops under the loop in order to twist it as it goes on the needle. What do you call this? Write that down so you remember it.

Also, be generous with the yarn here because you can tighten it after you place the loop on the left needle (see the tip below). I work a little away from the tip of the right needle, as shown, because I find it's easier. Do what's easiest for you.

Continue to cast on this way until you finish casting on the same number of stitches that were bound off for the buttonhole.

Tip: Don't immediately tighten the loop that you place on the left needle. First put the right needle between the two stitches on the left needle to start making another loop (as shown in the bottom picture on the previous page), then tighten the yarn. It's very hard to get the needle between those two stitches if you tighten the yarn first.

Now cable cast on one more stitch. But before you place this stitch on the left-hand needle, bring the yarn between the needles, from the back to the front.

Now place the final cast-on stitch on the needle, twisting it as you place it on the left needle. (Ignore the yarn you just brought from back to front, and twist this stitch like you twisted all the others.) Turn the work.

With yarn in back, slip the first stitch from the left needle to the right needle purlwise.

Use the left needle to pull the stitch that is second from the tip on the right needle over the stitch that is closest to the tip on the right needle, and pull it off the needle. This is the same action you do when binding off a stitch.

Now admire the beautiful buttonhole.

The word "horizontal" in the name of this buttonhole refers to the way it is created. You are working it horizontally in a row of the sweater band. But on the front band of a cardigan sweater, when the sweater is being worn, the buttonhole will actually be a vertical opening.

For Perfect Buttonholes, Plan Ahead

- **Buy the buttons before making the buttonholes.** It's easy to make the buttonholes fit the buttons. It's harder to find perfect buttons for your sweater if they also need to fit the buttonholes you've already made.

- **Make the buttonholes snug.** Even the one-row horizontal buttonhole, which is very firm, will stretch a little.

- **Always practice the buttonholes on your swatch to avoid the wear and tear of practicing on your sweater.** When I practice picking up stitches and knitting a band on my swatch, I practice the buttonholes, too. I make three different sizes of buttonholes: one I think will be the right size, one that is one stitch shorter, and one that is one stitch longer. For example, I'll make a three-stitch, a four-stitch, and a five-stitch buttonhole on the practice band on the swatch if I expect the four-stitch buttonhole to be the best. Then I'll test them with my buttons to see which size really is best. I'm looking for the one that's not too loose, not too snug, but just right.

Sewing Buttons onto the Band

To sew buttons onto a sweater, use sewing thread that matches the color of the sweater or the button. Although you could use yarn to sew on buttons, I've found that no matter how the yarn is tied or knotted, it eventually comes undone and works itself out of the buttons.

When attaching buttons, try to avoid sewing through the yarn. Instead, sew around the knit stitches, into the holes of the fabric. Sewing through the yarn will split it and weaken it. This may not matter in some sweaters, but if you have to remove the buttons when the sweater is washed, you want to be sure you aren't weakening the yarn every time you reattach the buttons.

Sew a flat button on the wrong side of the band behind each button. This stabilizes the fabric and prevents it from being pulled and stretched by frequent buttoning and unbuttoning. Attach both buttons at the same time, using the same piece of thread and sewing from back to front and front to back through both buttons.

Project Sweater

Work *Part 6* and *Part 7* of the Baby Cardi, on page 82, to pick up and knit stitches for the band, to work buttonholes, and to complete the sweater.

Good job! You have mastered the seven skills and now have the knowledge and confidence to make decisions about your knitting. Have fun with your next sweater project!

Patterns

Seven Sweaters

I have designed seven sweaters that use the techniques covered in the previous chapters. These sweaters are stylish, with interesting patterned edges, and are primarily stockinette stitch, which is simple to knit. There's not much going on in the knitting, so you can focus on the seven techniques you've just learned.

Only one sweater, the Baby Cardi, uses all seven techniques. But every sweater uses most of the techniques.

All of the sweaters include:

- Smooth or bumpy cast-on edge on public side
- Paired, slanting decreases
- Invisible increases
- Blocking
- Picking up stitches for bands.

Some of the sweaters include:

- Increasing in ribbing
- Buttonholes.

In the adult sweater patterns, the finished measurement is the bust measurement of the completed sweater as it will be worn, not the bust measurement of the person who will be wearing the sweater. The difference between the finished sweater bust measurement and the person's bust measurement is the wearing ease of the sweater. These sweaters are not skintight. Because you will wear blouses and tops under them, you must allow for wearing ease. The wearing ease on most of these sweaters is 2–6 inches, so read the pattern schematic carefully, take your measurements, and think about the way you like your sweaters to fit.

Be sure to read the Tips section at the end of each pattern for advice about seams and picking up stitches.

The Abbreviations and Terms appendix, directly following the patterns, is a reference source explaining abbreviations and terms used in the patterns. You can find information about seaming in the appendix about Techniques.

1. "Seven Things" Baby Cardi

This sweater, which fits a 6–12 month old child, includes all seven techniques. The pattern is divided into seven parts which correspond to the chapters of the book. You can read a chapter of the book, then knit the section of the sweater that uses the material you just learned.

This sweater is designed for a boy or girl, so use any color of yarn. When you finish the cardi, if you don't have someone to give it to, please donate it to a charity or a local hospital.

FINISHED MEASUREMENTS

Chest at Underarm (buttoned): 22"
Total Back Length: 10"

MATERIALS

2 skeins 220 Superwash from Cascade Yarns (100% superwash wool; 3.5oz/100g, 220yd/201m)
One pair each size 5 (3.75mm) and size 7 (4.5mm) needles or size needed to obtain gauge
Size 5 (3.75mm) circular needle (24" length)
Stitch holders
Four ¾" buttons
Tapestry needle

GAUGE

4.5 sts/1" and 6 rows/1" = 18 sts/4" and 24 rows/4" in Stockinette Stitch on larger needles, after blocking
To save time, take time to check gauge.

STITCH PATTERNS

K1 P1 Rib
(Even number of sts, selvage sts included)
Row 1 (RS): K1, *k1, p1; rep from * to last st, end k1.
Row 2: P1, *k1, p1; rep from * to last st, end p1.
Rep Rows 1 and 2 for patt.

Stockinette Stitch
(Any number of sts)
Row 1 (RS): Knit.

Row 2: Purl.

Rep Rows 1 and 2 for patt.

Part 1

BACK

With smaller needles, CO 46 sts.

Work in K1 P1 Rib for 1", ending after RS row.

Part 2

Inc 4 sts evenly on next rib row—50 sts.

Change to larger needles, beg Stockinette St and work even until piece measures 6" from beg, ending after WS row.

Part 3

Shape Armholes

BO 3 sts at beg of next two rows—44 sts.

Next Row (Dec Row—RS): K1, ssk, knit across until 3 sts rem, k2tog, k1—42 sts.

Rep Dec Row every RS row 2 more times—38 sts.

Work even until armholes measure 3", ending after WS row.

Divide for Neckline

K14, BO center 10 sts, k14. Work each side separately.

Left Neck Shaping

Dec Row 1 (WS): Purl across until 3 sts rem, ssp, p1—13 sts.

Dec Row 2: K1, ssk, knit across—12 sts.

Rep Dec Rows 1 and 2—10 sts.

Rep Dec Row 1—9 sts.

Place 9 sts on holder.

Right Neck Shaping

Attach yarn at neck edge on WS.

Dec Row 1 (WS): P1, p2tog, purl across—13 sts.

Dec Row 2: Knit across until 3 sts rem, k2tog, k1—12 sts.

Rep Dec Rows 1 and 2—10 sts.

Rep Dec Row 1—9 sts.

Place 9 sts on holder.

LEFT FRONT

With smaller needles, CO 20 sts.

Work in K1 P1 Rib for 1", ending after RS row.

Inc 2 sts evenly on next rib row—22 sts.

Change to larger needles, beg Stockinette St and work even until piece measures 6" from beg, ending after WS row.

Shape Armholes

BO 3 sts at beg of next row—19 sts.

Next Row (WS): Purl.

Continue to Shape Armholes *and at same time,* Shape Neck

Next Row (Dec Row—RS): K1, ssk, knit across until 3 sts rem, k2tog, k1—17 sts.

Rep Dec Row every RS row 2 more times—13 sts.

Next Row: Purl.

Continue working neck decreases as follows:

Next Row (Dec Row—RS): Knit across until 3 sts rem, k2tog, k1—12 sts.

Rep Dec Row every RS row 3 more times—9 sts.

Work even until armhole measures 4".

Place sts on holder.

RIGHT FRONT

Work as for Left Front to Shape Armholes, ending after RS row.

Shape Armholes

BO 3 sts at beg of next row—19 sts.

Continue to Shape Armholes *and at same time,* Shape Neck

Next Row (Dec Row—RS): K1, ssk, knit across until 3 sts rem, k2tog, k1—17 sts.

Rep Dec Row every RS row 2 more times—13 sts.

Next Row: Purl.

Continue working neck decreases as follows:

Next Row (Dec Row—RS): K1, ssk, knit across—12 sts.

Rep Dec Row every RS row 3 more times—9 sts.

Work even until armhole measures 4".

Place sts on holder.

Part 4

SLEEVE (make 2)

Sleeve to Underarm

With smaller needles, CO 28 sts.

Work in K1 P1 Rib for 1", ending after RS row.

Inc 2 sts evenly on next rib row—30 sts.

Change to larger needles, beg Stockinette St and work 8 rows even.

Next Row (Inc Row—RS): K1, M1 Right, knit across until one st rem, M1 Left, k1—32 sts.

Work Inc Row every 10th row 2 more times—36 sts.

Work even until piece measures $6\frac{1}{2}$" from beg, ending after WS row.

Shape Cap

BO 3 sts at beg of next 2 rows—30 sts.

Next Row (Dec Row—RS): K1, ssk, knit across until 3 sts rem, k2tog, k1—28 sts.

Rep Dec Row every RS row 9 more times—10 sts.

BO.

Part 5

FINISHING

Weave in all ends.

Block pieces to measurements.

Join shoulder sts using 3-needle BO. (For information on seams, see Techniques section.)

Sew seams to attach sleeves to body.

Sew side seams and sleeve seams.

Part 6 and Part 7

Place markers for four buttonholes on either right front edge (for a girl's sweater) or left front edge (for a boy's sweater). Place first marker ½ inch from bottom edge, and top marker at start of v-neck shaping. Space other two markers evenly between.

With RS facing and circular needle, beg at lower right front edge, pick up and knit 53 sts evenly along right front edge, 21 sts along back neck edge, and 53 sts along left front edge—127 sts total.

Work K1 P1 Rib edging as follows:

Row 1 (WS): P1, *k1, p1; rep from *.

Row 2: K1, *p1, k1; rep from *.

Row 3: Rep Row 1.

Row 4: Rep Row 2, working buttonholes at markers.

Row 5: Rep Row 1.

Row 6: Rep Row 2.

BO in patt.

Sew buttons to sweater on front edge opposite buttonholes.

TIP:

The number of stitches picked up for the edging must be an odd number.

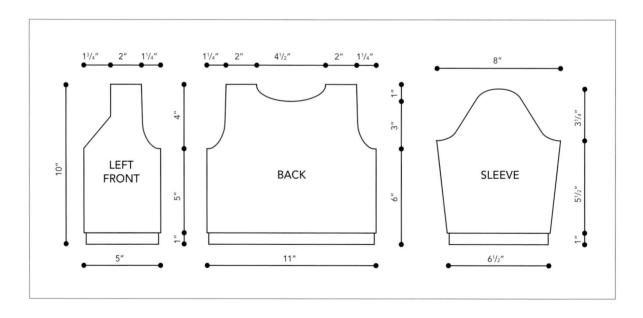

2. Diamond Yoke Pullover

This stockinette stitch pullover with a patterned yoke is fun to knit and to wear. The ribbed edgings and modified drop-shoulder style make it a comfortable, casual sweater. On the front and back, start with the ribbing, increasing in the last rib row, then decrease across the last stockinette stitch row before starting the yoke. The Diamond Brocade, a very popular stitch pattern, is a simple combination of knit and purl stitches. I have created a complete yoke chart for each size, to make the knitting easy.

The sweater length is designed to fall just below the waist. If you want a longer sweater, buy one more skein of yarn and knit two more inches of stockinette stitch before shaping the armholes.

FINISHED MEASUREMENTS

Bust: 38 (42, 46, 50)"
Total Back Length: 21 (21½ , 22, 23)"

MATERIALS

13 (14, 16, 17) skeins 1824 Wool from Mission
 Falls (100% merino superwash; 1.75oz/50g,
 85yd/78m) color Raspberry #029
One pair size 6 (4mm) needles or size needed to
 obtain gauge
Size 6 (4mm) circular needle (16" length)
Tapestry needle

GAUGE

4.5 sts/1" and 6 rows/1" = 18 sts/4" and 24 rows/4"
 in Stockinette Stitch, after blocking
4.25 sts/1" and 7.25 rows/1" = 17 sts/4" and
 29 rows/4" in Diamond Brocade Pattern
 (See Charts A–D), after blocking
To save time, take time to check gauge.

STITCH PATTERNS

K1 P1 Rib
(Even number of sts, selvage sts included)
Row 1 (RS): K1, *k1, p1; rep from * to last st,
 end k1.
Row 2: P1, *k1, p1; rep from * to last st, end p1.
Rep Rows 1 and 2 for patt.

Stockinette Stitch

(Any number of sts)

Row 1 (RS): Knit.

Row 2: Purl.

Rep Rows 1 and 2 for patt.

BACK

CO 82 (92, 100, 110) sts. Beg K1 P1 Rib and work for 1½", ending after RS row.

Inc 4 sts evenly on next row—86 (96, 104, 114) sts. Beg Stockinette St and work even until piece measures 12½ (12½, 12½, 13)" from beg, ending after WS row.

Shape Armholes

BO 8 (10, 11, 13) sts at the beg of the next 2 rows—70 (76, 82, 88).

Work even until armholes measure 2¼", ending after WS row.

Next Row (RS): Dec 3 (5, 5, 5) sts evenly across row—67 (71, 77, 83) sts.

Next Row: P1, knit across until 1 st rem, p1.

Beg Chart Patt for Yoke

Next Row (RS): Beg chart patt. Work even, following chart A (B, C, D), until 45 (49, 53, 57) rows have been completed—piece measures 21 (21½ , 22, 23)" from beg.

BO all sts purlwise.

Note: There is no neck shaping for the Back Yoke.

FRONT

Work as for back to Beg Chart Patt for Yoke.

Next Row (RS): Beg chart patt A (B, C, D). Shape neckline according to chart, binding off center sts on WS as indicated and working each side separately. For neckline shaping, work slanting decreases on edge stitches; ssk on Right Front neckline, k2tog on Left Front neckline. Work edge stitches around neckline (selvage stitches) in Stockinette St.

Work even until 45 (49, 53, 57) rows have been completed—piece measures 21 (21½ , 22, 23)" from beg.

BO all sts purlwise.

SLEEVE (make 2)

CO 38 (44, 48, 48) sts. Beg K1 P1 Rib and work for 1½", ending after RS row.

Inc 2 sts evenly on next row—40 (46, 50, 50) sts.

Beg Stockinette St and work 2 rows even.

Next Row (Inc Row—RS): K1, M1 Right, knit across until one st rem, M1 Left, k1—42 (48, 52, 52) sts.

Work Inc Row every every 4th row 2 (2, 2, 8) more times, then every 6th row 15 (15, 15, 11) times—76 (82, 86, 90) sts.

Work even until piece measures 20¼ (20¾ , 21, 21¼)" from beg, ending after WS row.

BO all sts knitwise.

FINISHING

Weave in all ends.

Block pieces to measurements.

Sew shoulder seams.

Sew seams to attach sleeves to body.

Sew side seams and sleeve seams.

Neckband

With RS facing and circular needle, beg at right shoulder and pick up and knit 82 (82, 84, 90) sts evenly along neck edge. Place marker, join and work in rounds as follows:

Round 1: *K1, p1, rep from *.

Rep Round 1 until band measures 1½".

BO in patt.

TIP:

The number of stitches picked up for the neckband must be a multiple of two.

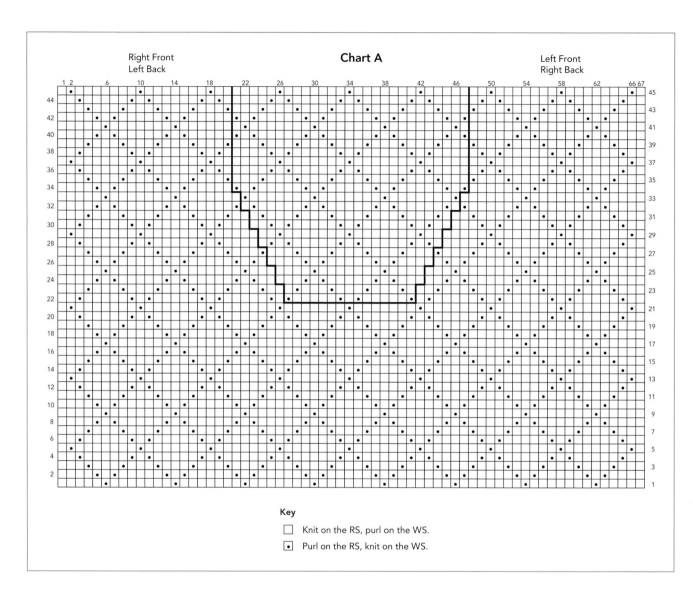

Right Front
Left Back

Chart A

Left Front
Right Back

Key

☐ Knit on the RS, purl on the WS.

⊡ Purl on the RS, knit on the WS.

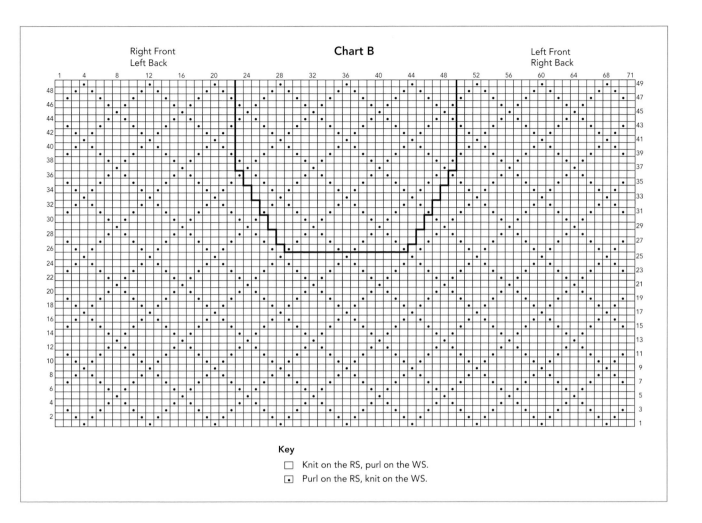

Key

☐ Knit on the RS, purl on the WS.

⊡ Purl on the RS, knit on the WS.

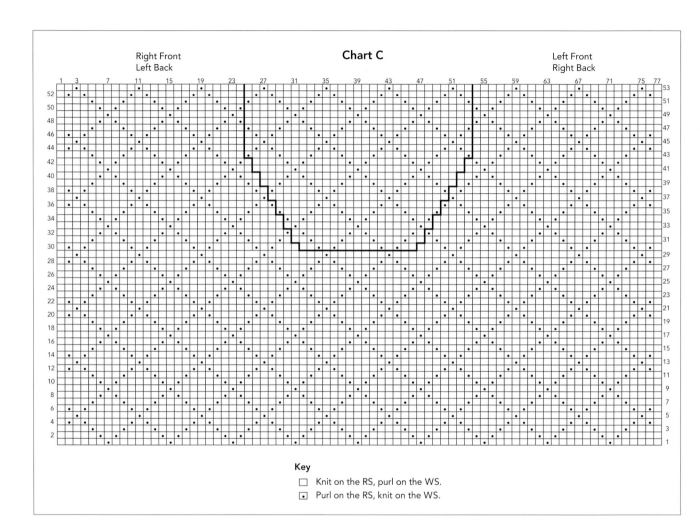

Chart C

Right Front
Left Back

Left Front
Right Back

Key

☐ Knit on the RS, purl on the WS.
⊡ Purl on the RS, knit on the WS.

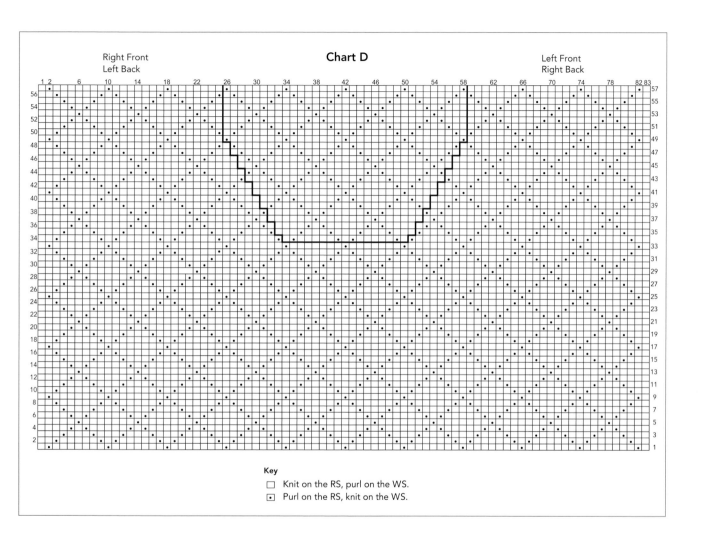

Chart D

Right Front
Left Back

Left Front
Right Back

Key

☐ Knit on the RS, purl on the WS.

⊡ Purl on the RS, knit on the WS.

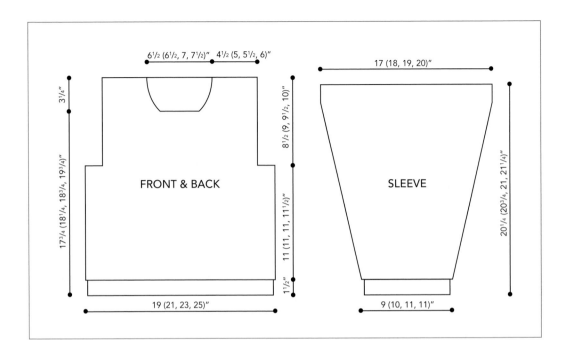

6½ (6½, 7, 7½)" 4½ (5, 5½, 6)"

3¼"

8½ (9, 9½, 10)"

17 (18, 19, 20)"

FRONT & BACK

SLEEVE

17¾ (18¼, 18¾, 19¾)"

11 (11, 11, 11½)"

1½"

20¼ (20¾, 21, 21¼)"

19 (21, 23, 25)"

9 (10, 11, 11)"

3. Eugenie's Cardigan

This classic, set-in sleeve cardigan has three top buttons for a updated look and fit. The armholes and neckline have full fashioned shaping, which you should feel free to change now that you know the options. The edging looks like a rib, but does not have the elasticity of ribbing due to the garter stitch sections between the knit stitches. It's really more like a border. Three buttonholes are worked in the top of the right front band.

In this pattern and in the pictured sweater, the decreases were placed three stitches from the edge, slanting in the same direction as the slant of the edge.

FINISHED MEASUREMENTS

Bust (buttoned): 38 (40, 44, 48)"
Length: 22 (22½ , 24, 24½)"

MATERIALS

5 (5, 6, 6) skeins Cascade 220 from Cascade Yarns (100% wool; 3.5oz/100g, 220yd/201m) color Amethyst Heather #9453

One pair size 6 (4mm) needles or size needed to obtain gauge

Size 6 (4mm) circular needle (24" length)

Three ⅞" buttons

Tapestry needle

GAUGE

4.5 sts/1" and 6 rows/1" = 18 sts/4" and 24 rows/4" in Stockinette Stitch, after blocking

To save time, take time to check gauge.

STITCH PATTERNS

Garter Stitch Rib—variation

(Multiple of 6 sts plus 3, selvage sts included)

Row 1 (WS): P3, *k3, p3; rep from * across.

Row 2: Knit.

Rep Rows 1 and 2 for patt.

Stockinette Stitch

(Any number of sts)

Row 1 (RS): Knit.

Row 2: Purl.

Rep Rows 1 and 2 for patt.

BACK

CO 93 (99, 111, 117) sts. Beg Garter Stitch Rib and work for 1½", ending after WS row.

Dec 7 (9, 11, 9) sts evenly on next row—86 (90, 100, 108) sts. **(Tip: Work k2tog decs in garter stitch sections of pattern.)**

Beg Stockinette St and work even until piece measures 13 (13, 13½, 13½)" from beg, ending after WS row.

Shape Armholes

BO 6 (6, 7, 9) sts at beg of next 2 rows—74 (78, 86, 90) sts.

Next Row (Dec Row—RS): K3, ssk, knit across until 5 sts rem, k2tog, k3—72 (76, 84, 88) sts.

Rep Dec Row every RS row 4 (4, 6, 7) more times—64 (68, 72, 74) sts.

Work even until armholes measure 8 (8½, 9½, 10)", ending after WS row.

Divide for Neckline

K23 (24, 26, 26), BO center 18 (20, 20, 22) sts, k23 (24, 26, 26). Work each side separately.

Shape Left Neck *and at same time,* Shape Shoulders

Row 1 (WS): Purl.

Row 2: K3, ssk, knit across—22 (23, 25, 25) sts.

Row 3: BO 7 (7, 8, 8) sts, purl across until 5 sts rem, ssp, p3—14 (15, 16, 16) sts.

Row 4: K3, ssk, knit across—13 (14, 15, 15) sts.

Row 5: BO 6 (7, 7, 7) sts, purl across until 5 sts rem, ssp, p3—6 (6, 7, 7) sts.

Row 6: Knit.

BO.

Shape Right Neck *and at same time,* Shape Shoulders

Attach yarn at neck edge on WS.

Row 1 (WS): Purl.

Row 2: BO 7 (7, 8, 8) sts, knit across until 5 sts rem, k2tog, k3—15 (16, 17, 17) sts.

Row 3: P3, p2tog, purl across—14 (15, 16, 16) sts.

Row 4: BO 6 (7, 7, 7) sts, knit across until 5 sts rem, k2tog, k3—7 (7, 8, 8) sts.

Row 5: P3, p2tog, purl across—6 (6, 7, 7) sts.

BO.

LEFT FRONT

With smaller needles, CO 45 (45, 51, 57) sts. Beg Garter Stitch Rib and work for 1½", ending after WS row.

Dec 5 (3, 5, 7) sts evenly on next row—40 (42, 46, 50) sts. **(Tip: Work k2tog decs in garter stitch sections of pattern.)**

Beg Stockinette St and work even until piece measures 13 (13, 13½, 13½)" from beg, ending after WS row.

Shape Armholes

BO 6 (6, 7, 9) sts at beg of next row—34 (36, 39, 41) sts.

Next Row: Purl.

Next Row (Dec Row—RS): K3, ssk, knit across—33 (35, 38, 40) sts.

Rep Dec Row every RS row 4 (4, 6, 7) more times—29 (31, 32, 33) sts.

Work even until armhole measures 5 (5½, 6½, 7)", ending after RS row.

Shape Neck

BO 5 sts at beg of next row—24 (26, 27, 28) sts.

Next Row (Dec Row—RS): Knit across until 5 sts rem, k2tog, k3—23 (25, 26, 27) sts.

Rep Dec Row every RS row 4 (5, 4, 5) more times—19 (20, 22, 22) sts.

Work even until neck measures 3¼", ending after WS row.

Shape Shoulder

Row 1 (RS): BO 7 (7, 8, 8) sts, knit across—12 (13, 14, 14) sts.

Row 2: Purl.

Row 3: BO 6 (7, 7, 7) sts, knit across—6 (6, 7, 7) sts.

Row 4: Purl.

BO.

RIGHT FRONT

Work as for Left Front to Shape Armholes, ending after RS row.

Shape Armholes

BO 6 (6, 7, 9) sts at beg of next row—34 (36, 39, 41) sts.

Next Row (Dec Row—RS): Knit across until 5 sts rem, k2tog, k3—33 (35, 38, 40) sts.

Rep Dec Row every RS row 4 (4, 6, 7) more times—29 (31, 32, 33) sts.

Work even until armhole measures 5 (5½, 6½, 7)", ending after WS row.

Shape Neck

BO 5 sts at beg of next row—24 (26, 27, 28) sts.

Next Row: Purl.

Next Row (Dec Row—RS): K3, ssk, knit across—23 (25 26, 27) sts.

Rep Dec Row every RS row 4 (5, 4, 5) more times—19 (20, 22, 22) sts.

Work even until neck measures 3¼", ending after RS row.

Shape Shoulder

Row 1 (WS): BO 7 (7, 8, 8) sts, purl across—12 (13, 14, 14) sts.

Row 2: Knit.

Row 3: BO 6 (7, 7, 7) sts, purl across—6 (6, 7, 7) sts.

Row 4: Knit.

BO.

SLEEVE (make 2)

Sleeve to Underarm

With smaller needles, CO 45 (45, 51, 57) sts. Beg Garter Stitch Rib and work for 1½", ending after WS row.

Dec 7 (5, 7, 7) sts evenly on next row—38 (40, 44, 50) sts. **(Tip: Work k2tog decs in garter stitch sections of pattern.)**

Beg Stockinette St and work even until piece measures 2½" from beg, ending after WS row.

Next Row (Inc Row—RS): K1, M1 Right, knit across until 1 st rem, M1 Left, k1—40 (42, 46, 52) sts.

Work Inc Row every 4th row 4 (7, 5, 2) more times, then every 6th row 8 (6, 8, 10) times—64 (68, 72, 76) sts.

Work even until piece measures 15 (15, 15$\frac{1}{2}$, 15$\frac{1}{2}$)" from beg, ending after WS row.

Shape Cap

BO 6 (6, 7, 9) sts at beg of next 2 rows—52 (56, 58, 58) sts.

Next Row (Dec Row—RS): K3, ssk, knit across until 5 sts rem, k2tog, k3—50 (54, 56, 56) sts.

Rep Dec Row every 4th row 0 (0, 0, 2) more times, then every other row 16 (14, 19, 17) times—18 (26, 18, 18) sts.

Decrease every row 0 (4, 0, 0) times, working RS Dec Rows as above and working WS Dec Rows as follows: P3, p2tog, purl across until 5 sts rem, ssp, p3—18 sts.

BO.

FINISHING

Weave in all ends.

Block pieces to measurements.

Sew shoulder seams.

Sew seams to attach sleeves to body.

Sew side seams and sleeve seams.

Neck Edging

With RS facing and circular needle, beg at top right front edge, pick up and knit 77 (83, 83, 83) sts evenly along neck edge. Work Garter Stitch Rib edging as follows:

Row 1 (WS): P4, *k3, p3; rep from *, end last repeat p4.

Row 2: Knit.

Rep Rows 1 and 2 until edging measures 1$\frac{1}{2}$".

BO in patt.

Left Front Edging

With RS facing and circular needle, beg at top left front edge, pick up and knit 99 (99, 111, 111) sts evenly along left front edge. Work Garter Stitch Rib (follow instructions under Stitch Patterns section) for 1$\frac{1}{2}$" (9 rows). BO in patt.

Right Front Edging

Place markers for three buttonholes on right front edge. Place first marker $\frac{1}{2}$ inch from top edge. Place bottom marker 4$\frac{1}{2}$" below first marker. Place third marker evenly between those two.

With RS facing and circular needle, beg at bottom right front edge, pick up and knit 99 (99, 111, 111) sts evenly along right front edge. Work as for Left Front Edging, working buttonholes at markers on 6th row.

Sew buttons to sweater on Left Front opposite buttonholes.

TIPS:

To seam the Garter Stitch Rib edging so the pattern is not interrupted, use the Mattress Stitch technique. Ignore the selvage stitches (the edge stitches), and sew into the center of the knit stitches next to the selvage stitches. The seam allowance is 1$\frac{1}{2}$ stitches on each side.

To seam the Stockinette Stitch above the edging, use Mattress Stitch placing one stitch (not 1$\frac{1}{2}$ stitches) in the seam allowance.

When picking up stitches for the neck edging, be sure to pick up a multiple of 6 plus 5.

When picking up stitches for the front edgings, be sure to pick up a multiple of 6 plus 3.

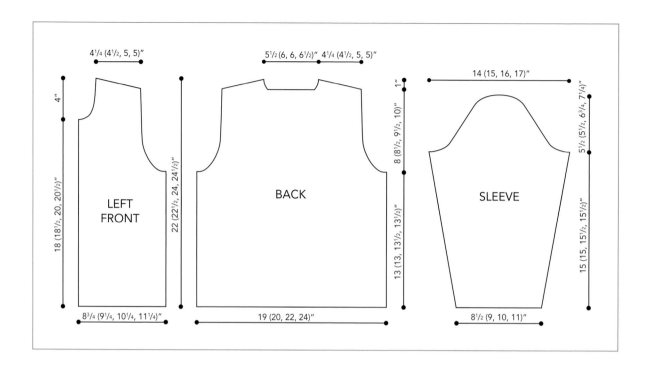

4¹/₄ (4¹/₂, 5, 5)"

5¹/₂ (6, 6, 6¹/₂)" 4¹/₄ (4¹/₂, 5, 5)"

14 (15, 16, 17)"

4"

1"

8 (8¹/₂, 9¹/₂, 10)"

5¹/₂ (5¹/₂, 6³/₄, 7¹/₄)"

22 (22¹/₂, 24, 24¹/₂)"

18 (18¹/₂, 20, 20¹/₂)"

13 (13, 13¹/₂, 13¹/₂)"

15 (15, 15¹/₂, 15¹/₂)"

LEFT FRONT

BACK

SLEEVE

8³/₄ (9¹/₄, 10¹/₄, 11¹/₄)"

19 (20, 22, 24)"

8¹/₂ (9, 10, 11)"

4. Two-Texture Pullover

I love textured fabrics, and who wouldn't look good in this pullover with lovely textured edgings? The patterned edging, a ribbing variation, contrasts nicely with the smooth stockinette stitch sweater. The shape is the same as the Diamond Yoke Pullover, but the look is entirely different since the texture is at the edges rather than at the yoke. Sleeve increases and neckline decreases are worked in stockinette stitch, and stitches are picked up and knit for the textured neckband.

As with the Diamond Yoke Pullover, the sweater length is designed to fall just below the waist. If you want a longer sweater, buy one more skein of yarn and knit two more inches of stockinette stitch before shaping the armholes.

FINISHED MEASUREMENTS

Bust: 38 (42, 46, 50)"
Total Back Length: 21 (21½ , 22, 23)"

MATERIALS

13 (14, 16, 17) skeins 1824 Wool from Mission Falls (100% merino superwash; 1.75oz/50g, 85yd/78m) color Macaw #027
One pair size 6 (4mm) needles or size needed to obtain gauge
Size 6 (4mm) circular needle (16" length)
Stitch marker
Tapestry needle

GAUGE

5 sts/1" and 6.5 rows/1" = 20 sts/4" and 26 rows/4" in Garter Ridge Rib, after blocking
4.5 sts/in and 6 rows/in = 18 sts/4" and 24 rows/4" in Stockinette Stitch, after blocking
To save time, take time to check gauge.

STITCH PATTERNS

Garter Ridge Rib—variation
(Multiple of 3 sts plus 2, selvage sts included)
Row 1 (RS): K2, *p1, k2; rep from * to end.
Row 2: P2, *k1, p2; rep from * to end.
Row 3: K2, *p1, k2; rep from * to end.
Row 4: P1, knit across until 1 st rem, p1.
Rep Rows 1–4 for patt.

Stockinette Stitch

(Any number of sts)

Row 1 (RS): Knit.

Row 2: Purl.

Rep Rows 1 and 2 for patt.

BACK

CO 95 (107, 116, 125) sts. Beg Garter Ridge Rib and work for 5$\frac{1}{2}$", ending after Row 4.

Beg Stockinette St and dec 9 (11, 12, 11) sts evenly on next row—86 (96, 104, 114) sts.

Work even until piece measures 12$\frac{1}{2}$ (12$\frac{1}{2}$, 12$\frac{1}{2}$, 13)" from beg, ending after WS row.

Shape Armholes

BO 8 (10, 11, 13) sts at the beg of the next 2 rows—70 (76, 82, 88) sts.

Work even until armholes measure 8$\frac{1}{2}$ (9, 9$\frac{1}{2}$, 10)".

BO.

FRONT

Work as for back to Shape Armholes.

Shape Armholes

BO 8 (10, 11, 13) sts at the beg of the next 2 rows—70 (76, 82, 88) sts.

Work even until armhole measures 5$\frac{1}{4}$ (5$\frac{3}{4}$, 6$\frac{1}{4}$, 6$\frac{3}{4}$)", ending after WS row.

Divide for Neckline

K27 (30, 33, 35), BO center 16 (16, 16, 18) sts, k27 (30, 33, 35). Work each side separately.

Shape Right Neck

Next Row (WS): Purl.

Next Row (Dec Row—RS): K1, ssk, knit across— 26 (29, 32, 34) sts.

Rep Dec Row every RS row 6 (6, 7, 7) more times—20 (23, 25, 27) sts.

Work even until neck measures 3$\frac{1}{4}$".

BO.

Shape Left Neck

Attach yarn at neck edge on WS.

Next Row (WS): Purl.

Next Row (Dec Row—RS): Knit across until 3 sts rem, k2tog, k1—26 (29, 32, 34) sts.

Rep Dec Row every RS row 6 (6, 7, 7) more times—20 (23, 25, 27) sts.

Work even until neck measures 3$\frac{1}{4}$".

BO.

SLEEVE (make 2)

CO 47 (50, 56, 56) sts. Beg Garter Ridge Rib and work for 5$\frac{1}{2}$", ending after Row 4.

Beg Stockinette St and dec 7 (4, 6, 6) sts evenly on next row—40 (46, 50, 50) sts.

Work 3 (3, 3, 1) rows even.

Next Row (Inc Row—RS): K1, M1 Right, knit across until 1 st rem, M1 Left, k1—42 (48, 52, 52) sts.

Work Inc Row every other row 0 (0, 0, 4) more times, then every 4th row 17 (17, 17, 15) times—76 (82, 86, 90) sts.

Work even until piece measures 20¼ (20¾, 21, 21¼)" from beg.

BO.

FINISHING

Weave in all ends.

Block pieces to measurements.

Sew shoulder seams.

Sew seams to attach sleeves to body.

Sew side seams and sleeve seams.

Neckband

With RS facing and circular needle, beg at right shoulder, pick up and knit 84 (84, 87, 93) sts evenly along neck edge. Place marker, join and work in Garter Ridge Rib rounds as follows:

Round 1: Purl.

Rounds 2, 3 and 4: *K2, p1; rep from * around.

Rep Rounds 1–4.

BO all sts purlwise.

> **TIP:**
>
> *The number of stitches picked up for the neckband must be a multiple of three.*

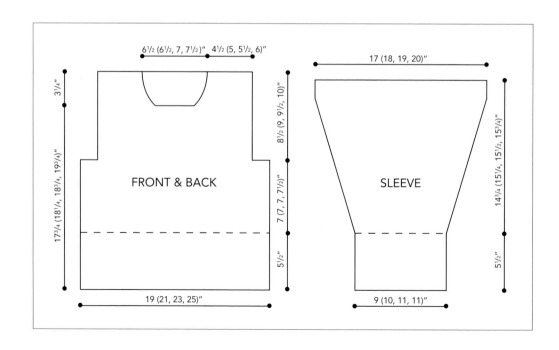

5. Sweater without Sleeves

I live near Washington, D.C. Although many winter days are mild, occasionally we get snow and sometimes the temperature is very cold. In the winter, my husband likes to keep the thermostat turned down low in our house to save energy. One year, on a very cold day in December, I was wearing one of my hand knit vests, but I still felt cold. I said to my husband, "I'm cold." And he said to me, "Why don't you put on a sweater?" He always says that when I tell him I'm cold. "I am wearing a sweater," I replied. And he said, "Why don't you knit a sweater that has sleeves?"

I like vests because they are comfortable and stylish and can be worn in different seasons and climates. In this "sweater without sleeves," the square neckline and textured yoke add pizzaz to a simple stockinette stitch vest. The finishing is minimal with two buttonholes and a one-row edging on the fronts.

FINISHED MEASUREMENTS

Bust (buttoned): 36 (40, 44, 48)"
Length: 20 (20½ , 21, 21½)"

MATERIALS

3 (3, 3, 4) skeins Cascade 220 from Cascade Yarns (100% wool; 3.5oz/100g, 220yd/201m), color Turquoise #9468
One pair size 6 (4mm) needles or size needed to obtain gauge
Size 4 (3.5mm) circular needle (24" length)
Stitch holders
Two ¾" buttons
Tapestry needle

GAUGE

5 sts/1" and 7 rows/1" = 20 sts/4" and 28 rows/4" in Rice Stitch on larger needles, after blocking
4.5 sts/1" and 6 rows/1" = 18 sts/4" and 24 rows/4" in Stockinette Stitch on larger needles, after blocking
To save time, take time to check gauge.

STITCH PATTERNS

Rice Stitch

(Odd number of sts, selvage sts included)

Row 1 (RS): P1, *k1 through the back loop, p1; rep from * to end.

Row 2: Knit.

Rep Rows 1 and 2 for patt.

Stockinette Stitch

(Any number of sts)

Row 1 (RS): Knit.

Row 2: Purl.

Rep Rows 1 and 2 for patt.

BACK

With larger needles, CO 81 (89, 99, 107) sts. Beg Rice St and work 5 rows even.

Next Row (WS): K40 (44, 49, 53), M1 Right, k41 (45, 50, 54)—82 (90, 100, 108) sts.

Beg Stockinette St and work even until piece measures 11½" from beg, ending after WS row.

Shape Armholes

BO 6 (7, 9, 10) sts at beg of next 2 rows—70 (76, 82, 88) sts.

Next Row (Dec Row—RS): K1, ssk, knit across until 3 sts rem, k2tog, k1—68 (74, 80, 86) sts.

Rep Dec Row every RS row 4 (6, 7, 8) more times, ending after RS row—60 (62, 66, 70) sts.

Yoke

Next Row (Inc Row—WS): Knit, increasing 7 sts evenly across row (use bar increase)—67 (69, 73, 77) sts.

Beg Rice Stitch and work even until armholes measure 7½ (8, 8½, 9)", ending after WS row.

Divide for Neckline

Work 19 (19, 21, 23) sts, BO center 29 (31, 31, 31) sts, work 19 (19, 21, 23) sts. Work each side separately.

Left Neck

Work 5 rows even.

Place stitches on holder.

Right Neck

Attach yarn at neck edge on WS.

Work 5 rows even.

Place stitches on holder.

LEFT FRONT

With larger needles, CO 41 (45, 49, 53) sts. Beg Rice St and work 5 rows even.

Next Row (WS): K20 (22, 24, 26), M1 Right, k21 (23, 25, 27)—42 (46, 50, 54) sts.

Beg Stockinette St and work even until piece measures 11½" from beg, ending after WS row.

Shape Armhole

BO 6 (7, 9, 10) sts at beg of next row—36 (39, 41, 44) sts.

Next Row: Purl.

Next Row (Dec Row—RS): K1, ssk, knit across—35 (38, 40, 43) sts.

Rep Dec Row every RS row 4 (6, 7, 8) more times, ending after RS row—31 (32, 33, 35) sts.

Yoke

Next Row (Inc Row—WS): Knit, increasing 2 (3, 4, 4) sts evenly across row (use bar increase)—33 (35, 37, 39) sts.

Beg Rice Stitch and work even until armhole measures 5 (5½, 6, 6½)" ending after RS row.

Shape Neck

Next Row: BO 14 (16, 16, 16) sts, work across in patt as estab—19 (19, 21, 23) sts.

Work in patt as estab until armhole measures 8½ (9, 9½, 10)", ending after WS row.

Place stitches on holder.

RIGHT FRONT

Work as for Left Front to Shape Armholes, ending after RS row.

Shape Armhole

BO 6 (7, 9, 10) sts at beg of next row—36 (39, 41, 44) sts.

Next Row (Dec Row—RS): Knit across until 3 sts rem, k2tog, k1—35 (38, 40, 43) sts.

Rep Dec Row every RS row 4 (6, 7, 8) more times, ending after RS row—31 (32, 33, 35) sts.

Yoke

Next Row (Inc Row—WS): Knit, increasing 2 (3, 4, 4) sts evenly across row (use bar increase)—33 (35, 37, 39) sts.

Beg Rice Stitch and work even until armhole measures 5 (5½, 6, 6½)" ending after WS row.

Shape Neck

Next Row: BO 14 (16, 16, 16) sts, work across in patt as estab—19 (19, 21, 23) sts.

Work in patt as estab until armhole measures 8½ (9, 9½, 10)", ending after WS row.

Place stitches on holder.

FINISHING

Weave in all ends.

Block pieces to measurements.

Join shoulder sts using 3-needle BO.

Sew side seams.

Left Front Edging

Measure out 4 yds of yarn from the ball. Start at this place to use yarn to pick up and knit stitches, using yarn in direction toward tail—not in the direction toward the ball. With RS facing and circular needle, beg at top left front edge, pick up and knit 74 (78, 82, 82) sts evenly along left front edge. Do not turn. Slide stitches to opposite end of needle, use attached yarn (which goes to the ball), and work as follows:

Next Row (RS): Knit across row. Turn.

With WS facing, BO all sts knitwise.

Right Front Edging

Place markers for two buttonholes on right front edge of yoke. Place first marker ½" below neckline edge, and place second marker ½" above Yoke's lower edge.

Work with yarn as for Left Front Edging above. With RS facing and circular needle, beg at lower right front edge, pick up and knit 74 (78, 82, 82) sts evenly along right front edge. Do not turn. Slide stitches to opposite end of needle, use attached yarn and work as follows:

Next Row (RS): Knit, working buttonholes at markers. Turn.

With WS facing, BO all sts knitwise.

Sew buttons to sweater on Left Front opposite buttonholes.

> **TIP:**
>
> *To seam vertical edges of Rice Stitch, use same technique as for Invisible Seam on Reverse Stockinette and sew through edge stitches.*

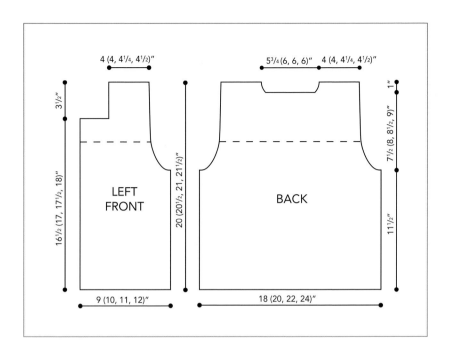

4 (4, 4¼, 4½)"

5¾ (6, 6, 6)"   4 (4, 4¼, 4½)"

3½"

16½ (17, 17½, 18)"

20 (20½, 21, 21½)"

7½ (8, 8½, 9)"   1"

11½"

LEFT FRONT

BACK

9 (10, 11, 12)"

18 (20, 22, 24)"

6. Color Tie Cardigan

This sweater combines fuchsia, black and lime green for a visual punch. The sweater is worked in stockinette stitch, but the color blocks make it interesting. The sweater is slightly fitted with decreases between the hip and the waist and increases between the waist and the bust. For the shaping, you can follow the pattern or make your own decision about the type and placement of the increases and decreases. Near the edges or full fashioned? Slanting with or against the angle of the edge? It's your sweater, so you get to decide.

In this pattern and in the pictured sweater, all decreases and increases were placed one stitch from the edge, slanting in the same direction as the slant of the edge.

FINISHED MEASUREMENTS

Bust (buttoned): 38 (40, 44, 48)"
Total Back Length: 22 (22½, 23½, 24)"

MATERIALS

Lamb's Pride Worsted from Brown Sheep Company (85% wool/15% mohair; 4oz/113g, 190yd/173m)
2 (2, 2, 3) skeins Limeade (A)
2 (2, 2, 3) skeins Onyx (B)
2 (2, 2, 3) skeins Lotus Pink (C)
One pair each size 5 (3.75mm) and 7 (4.5mm) needles or size needed to obtain gauge
Size 5 (3.75mm) circular needle (24" length)
Size 5 (3.75mm) double-pointed needles
Tapestry needle

GAUGE

4.25 sts/1" and 5.75 rows/1" = 17 sts/4" and 23 rows/4" in Stockinette Stitch on larger needles, after blocking
To save time, take time to check gauge.

STITCH PATTERNS

Garter Stitch
(Any number of sts)
Row 1 (RS): Knit.

Row 2: Knit.

Rep Rows 1 and 2 for patt.

Stockinette Stitch

(Any number of sts)

Row 1 (RS): Knit.

Row 2: Purl.

Rep Rows 1 and 2 for patt.

LEFT BACK

With smaller needles and B, CO 40 (42, 46, 52) sts. Beg Garter St and work 4 rows even.

Change to larger needles and A, beg Stockinette St and work until piece measures 2" from beg, ending after WS row.

Decrease for Waist

Next row (Dec Row—RS): Knit across until 3 sts rem, k2tog, k1—39 (41, 45, 51) sts.

Work even until piece measures 4" from beg, ending after WS row.

Rep Dec Row—38 (40, 44, 50) sts.

Work even until piece measures 7" from beg, ending after WS row.

Increase for Bust

Next row (Inc Row—RS): Knit across until 1 st rem, M1 Left, k1—39 (41, 45, 51) sts.

Work even until piece measures 10" from beg, ending after WS row.

Rep Inc Row—40 (42, 46, 52) sts.

Work even until piece measures 13 (13, 13$\frac{1}{2}$, 13$\frac{1}{2}$)" from beg, ending after RS row.

Shape Armhole

BO 5 (5, 7, 9) sts at beg of next row—35 (37, 39, 43) sts.

Next Row (Dec Row—RS): Knit across until 3 sts rem, k2tog, k1—34 (36, 38, 42) sts.

Work Dec Row every RS row 3 (4, 5, 8) more times—31 (32, 33, 34) sts.

Work even until armhole measures 7$\frac{1}{2}$ (8, 8$\frac{1}{2}$, 9)", ending after WS row.

Shape Neck

BO 8 (8, 8, 9) sts, knit across—23 (24, 25, 25) sts.

Next Row: Purl.

Next Row: K1, ssk, knit across—22 (23, 24, 24) sts.

Continue to Shape Neck *and at same time,* **Shape Shoulder**

Row 1 (WS): BO 7 sts, purl across until 3 sts rem, ssp, p1—14 (15, 16, 16) sts.

Row 2: K1, ssk, knit across—13 (14, 15, 15) sts.

Row 3: BO 6 (7, 7, 7) sts, purl across until 3 sts rem, ssp, p1—6 (6, 7, 7) sts.

Row 4: Knit.

BO.

RIGHT BACK

With smaller needles and C, CO 40 (42, 46, 52) sts. Beg Garter St and work 4 rows even.

Change to larger needles and B, beg Stockinette St and work until piece measures 2" from beg, ending after WS row.

Decrease for Waist

Next row (Dec Row—RS): K1, ssk, knit across—39 (41, 45, 51) sts.

Work even until piece measures 4" from beg, ending after WS row.

Rep Dec Row—38 (40, 44, 50) sts.

Work even until piece measures 7" from beg, ending after WS row.

Increase for Bust

Next row (Inc Row—RS): K1, M1 Right, knit across—39 (41, 45, 51) sts.

Work even until piece measures 10" from beg, ending after WS row.

Rep Inc Row—40 (42, 46, 52) sts.

Work even until piece measures 13 (13, 13½, 13½)" from beg, ending after WS row.

Shape Armhole

BO 5 (5, 7, 9) sts at beg of next row—35 (37, 39, 43) sts.

Next Row: Purl.

Next Row (Dec Row—RS): K1, ssk, knit across— 34 (36, 38, 42) sts.

Work Dec Row every RS row 3 (4, 5, 8) more times—31 (32, 33, 34) sts.

Work even until armhole measures 7½ (8, 8½, 9)", ending after RS row.

Shape Neck

BO 8 (8, 8, 9) sts, purl across—23 (24, 25, 25) sts.

Continue to Shape Neck *and at same time,* **Shape Shoulder**

Row 1 (RS): BO 7 sts, knit across until 3 sts rem, k2tog, k1—15 (16, 17, 17) sts.

Row 2: P1, p2tog, purl across—14 (15, 16, 16) sts.

Row 3: BO 6 (7, 7, 7) sts, knit across until 3 sts rem, k2tog, k1—7 (7, 8, 8) sts.

Row 4: P1, p2tog, purl across—6 (6, 7, 7) sts.

BO.

LEFT FRONT

With smaller needles and A, CO 38 (40, 44, 50) sts. Beg Garter St and work 4 rows even.

Change to larger needles and B, beg Stockinette St and work until piece measures 2" from beg, ending after WS row.

Decrease for Waist

Next row (Dec Row—RS): K1, ssk, knit across— 37 (39, 43, 49) sts.

Work even until piece measures 4" from beg, ending after WS row.

Rep Dec Row—36 (38, 42, 48) sts.

Work even until piece measures 7" from beg, ending after WS row.

Increase for Bust

Next row (Inc Row—RS): K1, M1 Right, knit across—37 (39, 43, 49) sts.

Work even until piece measures 10" from beg, ending after WS row.

Rep Inc Row—38 (40, 44, 50) sts.

Work even until piece measures 13 (13, 13½, 13½)" from beg, ending after WS row.

Shape Armhole *and at same time,* **Shape Neck**

Next Row (RS): BO 5 (5, 7, 9) sts, knit across until 3 sts rem, k2tog, k1—32 (34, 36, 40) sts.

Next Row: Purl.

Row 1 (Armhole Dec Row—RS): K1, ssk, knit across—31 (33, 35, 39) sts.

Row 2: Purl.

Row 3 (Armhole and Neck Dec Row—RS): K1, ssk, knit across until 3 sts rem, k2tog, k1—29 (31, 33, 37) sts.

Row 4: Purl.

Rep [Rows 1–4] 1 (1, 2, 3) more times—26 (28, 27, 28) sts.

Rep [Rows 1 and 2] 0 (1, 0, 1) more times—26 (27, 27, 27) sts.

Work 2 (0, 2, 0) rows even.

Next Row (Neck Dec Row—RS): Knit across until 3 sts rem, k2tog, k1—25 (26, 26, 26) sts.

Rep Neck Dec Row every 4th row 6 (6, 5, 5) more times—19 (20, 21, 21) sts.

Work even until armhole measures 8 (8½, 9, 9½)", ending after WS row.

Shape Shoulder

Row 1 (RS): BO 7 sts, knit across—12 (13, 14, 14) sts.

Row 2: Purl.

Row 3: BO 6 (7, 7, 7) sts, knit across—6 (6, 7, 7) sts.

Row 4: Purl.

BO.

RIGHT FRONT

With smaller needles and B, CO 38 (40, 44, 50) sts. Beg Garter St and work 4 rows even.

Change to larger needles and C, beg Stockinette St and work until piece measures 2" from beg, ending after WS row.

Decrease for Waist

Next row (Dec Row—RS): Knit across until 3 sts rem, k2tog, k1—37 (39, 43, 49) sts.

Work even until piece measures 4" from beg, ending after WS row.

Rep Dec Row—36 (38, 42, 48) sts.

Work even until piece measures 7" from beg, ending after WS row.

Increase for Bust

Next row (Inc Row—RS): Knit across until 1 st rem, M1 Left, k1—37 (39, 43, 49) sts.

Work even until piece measures 10" from beg, ending after WS row.

Rep Inc Row—38 (40, 44, 50) sts.

Work even until piece measures 13 (13, 13½, 13½)" from beg, ending after RS row.

Shape Armhole *and at same time,* Shape Neck

Next Row (WS): BO 5 (5, 7, 9) sts , purl across until 3 sts rem, ssp, p1—32 (34, 36, 40) sts.

Row 1 (Armhole Dec Row—RS): Knit across until 3 sts rem, k2tog, k1—31 (33, 35, 39) sts.

Row 2: Purl.

Row 3 (Armhole and Neck Dec Row—RS): K1, ssk, knit across until 3 sts rem, k2tog, k1—29 (31, 33, 37) sts.

Row 4: Purl.

Rep [Rows 1–4] 1 (1, 2, 3) more times—26 (28, 27, 28) sts.

Rep [Rows 1 and 2] 0 (1, 0, 1) more times—26 (27, 27, 27) sts.

Work 2 (0, 2, 0) rows even.

Next Row (Neck Dec Row—RS): K1, ssk, knit across—25 (26, 26, 26) sts.

Rep Neck Dec Row every 4th row 6 (6, 5, 5) more times—19 (20, 21, 21).

Work even until armhole measures 8 (8½, 9, 9½)", ending after RS row.

Shape Shoulder

Row 1 (WS): BO 7 sts, purl across—12 (13, 14, 14) sts.

Row 2: Knit.

Row 3: BO 6 (7, 7, 7) sts, purl across—6 (6, 7, 7) sts.

Row 4: Knit.

BO.

LEFT SLEEVE

Sleeve to Underarm

With smaller needles and A, CO 40 (40, 42, 42) sts. Beg Garter St and work 4 rows even.

Change to larger needles and C, beg Stockinette St, and work 2 rows even.

Next Row (Inc Row—RS): K1, M1 Right, knit across until 1 st rem, M1 Left, k1—42 (42, 44, 44) sts.

Rep Inc Row every 4th row 0 (0, 0, 3) more times, every 6th row 0 (6, 9, 11) times, then every 8th row 9 (5, 3, 0) times—60 (64, 68, 72) sts.

Work even until piece measures 15 (15½, 15½, 15¾)" from beg, ending after WS row.

Shape Cap

BO 5 (5, 7, 9) sts at beg of next 2 rows—50 (54, 54, 54) sts.

Work 2 rows even.

Next Row (Dec Row—RS): K1, ssk, knit across until 3 sts rem, k2tog, k1—48 (52, 52, 52) sts.

Rep Dec Row every 4th row 0 (0, 0, 1) more time, then every other row 13 (13, 19, 18) times—22 (26, 14, 14) sts.

Decrease every row 6 (8, 0, 0) times, working RS Dec Rows as above and working WS Dec Rows as follows: P1, p2tog, purl across until 3 sts rem, ssp, p1—10 (10, 14, 14) sts.

BO.

RIGHT SLEEVE

Work as for Left Sleeve, using C for CO and Garter St edging, then changing to A for Stockinette St.

FINISHING

Weave in all ends.

Block pieces to measurements.

Sew shoulders seams.

Left Front Edging

With RS facing, circular needle and C, beg at left center back edge, pick up and knit 13 (13, 13, 14) sts evenly along back neck edge and 102 (104, 108, 110) sts evenly along left front edge—115 (117, 121, 124) sts total. Work 4 rows in Garter St. BO in patt.

Right Front Edging

With RS facing, circular needle and A, beg at lower right front edge, pick up and knit 102 (104, 108, 110) sts evenly along right front edge and 13 (13, 13, 14) sts along back neck edge, ending at center back—115 (117, 121, 124) sts total. Work 4 rows in Garter St. BO in patt.

Sew back center seam.

Sew seams to attach sleeves to body.

Sew side seams and sleeve seams.

I-cord Ties

Place 4 markers for I-cord ties, 2 per side, along
front band. Place top marker 2" below start of
V-neck shaping, and bottom marker 2" below
top marker. At top marker on Right Front, with
RS facing, and using color B and dpn, pick up
and knit 3 sts. Work I-cord, as follows:

Knit 1 row. *Slide the stitches to the other end of
the needle without turning the work. Pull the
yarn tightly and knit 1 row. Rep from * until
I-cord measures 12". Cut tail, thread into
tapestry needle and draw through the 3 sts and
tighten. Weave in tail.

Work I-cord at other markers using color B at lower
Right Front marker. On Left Front, use color A
for both cords.

TIP:

*To seam the Garter St edging, use the Invisible
Seam on Reverse Stockinette Stitch technique.*

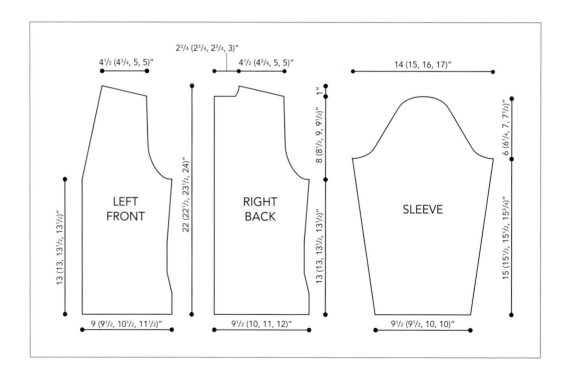

7. My Sister's Sweater

This warm sweater-jacket has wide textured bands, set-in sleeves, and a swing jacket shape and length. Make it for yourself, a friend, or for your sister in any color you like. I don't have to make one for my sister since, as a test knitter, she has already knit her own in a beautiful olive green.

The shaping in this pattern is not full fashioned, but you could certainly change that by moving the increases and decreases two or three stitches from the edge. The wide textured borders call for big buttons and as a result, big buttonholes.

FINISHED MEASUREMENTS

Bust (buttoned): 38 (42, 46, 50)"
Length: 26 (27, 27, 28)"

MATERIALS

6 (6, 7, 8) skeins Lamb's Pride Worsted from Brown Sheep Company (85% wool/15% mohair; 4oz/113g, 190yd/173m), color Mulberry #M-162

One pair each size 6 (4mm) needles and 7 (4.5mm) needles or sizes needed to obtain gauge

Size 6 (4mm) circular needle (24" length)

Three 1¹/₂" buttons

Tapestry needle

GAUGE

5 sts/1" and 7.5 rows/1" = 20 sts/4"and 30 rows/4" in Broken Rib on smaller needles, after blocking

4.25 sts/1" and 5.75 rows/1" = 17 sts/4"and 23 rows/4" in Stockinette Stitch on larger needles, after blocking

To save time, take time to check gauge.

STITCH PATTERNS

Broken Rib—variation
(Even number of sts, selvage sts included)
Row 1 (RS): K1, *k1, p1; rep from * to last st, k1.
Row 2: P1, knit across to last st, p1.
Rep Rows 1 and 2 for patt.

Stockinette Stitch

(Any number of sts)

Row 1 (RS): Knit.

Row 2: Purl.

Rep Rows 1 and 2 for patt.

BACK

With smaller needles, CO 102 (112, 122, 132) sts. Beg Broken Rib and work for 2½", ending after RS row.

Dec 12 (14, 16, 18) sts evenly on next row—90 (98, 106, 114) sts. (Use k2tog decrease.)

Change to larger needles, beg Stockinette St and work even until piece measures 5½" from beg, ending after WS row.

Shape Sides

Next Row (Dec Row—RS): K1, ssk, knit across until 3 sts rem, k2tog, k1—88 (96, 104, 112) sts.

Rep Dec Row every 18th row 3 more times—82 (90, 98, 106) sts.

Work even until piece measures 17" from beg, ending after WS row.

Shape Armholes

BO 6 (7, 9, 10) sts at beg of next 2 rows—70 (76, 80, 86) sts.

Next Row (Dec Row—RS): K1, ssk, knit across until 3 sts rem, k2tog, k1—68 (74, 78, 84) sts.

Rep Dec Row every RS row 4 (6, 7, 8) more times—60 (62, 64, 68) sts.

Work even until armholes measure 8 (9, 9, 10)", ending after WS row.

Divide for Neckline

K20 (20, 20, 22), BO center 20 (22, 24, 24) sts, k20 (20, 20, 22). Work each side separately.

Shape Left Neck *and at same time,* Shape Shoulders

Row 1 (WS): Purl.

Row 2: K1, ssk, knit across—19 (19, 19, 21) sts.

Row 3: BO 6 sts, purl across until 3 sts rem, ssp, p1—12 (12, 12, 14) sts.

Row 4: K1, ssk, knit across—11 (11, 11, 13) sts.

Row 5: BO 5 (5, 5, 6) sts, purl across until 3 sts rem, ssp, p1—5 (5, 5, 6) sts.

Row 6: Knit.

BO.

Shape Right Neck *and at same time,* Shape Shoulders

Attach yarn at neck edge on WS.

Row 1 (WS): Purl.

Row 2: BO 6 sts, knit across until 3 sts rem, k2tog, k1—13 (13, 13, 15) sts.

Row 3: P1, p2tog, purl across—12 (12, 12, 14) sts.

Row 4: BO 5 (5, 5, 6) sts, knit across until 3 sts rem, k2tog, k1—6 (6, 6, 7) sts.

Row 5: P1, p2tog, purl across—5 (5, 5, 6) sts.

BO.

LEFT FRONT

With smaller needles, CO 46 (50, 56, 60) sts. Beg Broken Rib and work for 2½", ending after RS row.

Dec 6 (6, 8, 8) sts evenly on next row—40 (44, 48, 52) sts. (Use k2tog decrease.)

Change to larger needles, beg Stockinette St and work even until piece measures 5½" from beg, ending after WS row.

Shape Sides

Next Row (Dec Row—RS): K1, ssk, knit across—39 (43, 47, 51) sts.

Rep Dec Row every 18th row 3 more times—36 (40, 44, 48) sts.

Work even until piece measures 17" from beg, ending after WS row.

Shape Armholes

BO 6 (7, 9, 10) sts at beg of next row—30 (33, 35, 38) sts.

Next Row: Purl.

Next Row (Dec Row—RS): K1, ssk, knit across—29 (32, 34, 37) sts.

Rep Dec Row every RS row 4 (6, 7, 8) more times—25 (26, 27, 29) sts.

Work even until armhole measures 6 (7, 7, 8)", ending after RS row.

Shape Neck

BO 4 (5, 6, 6) sts at beg of next row—21 (21, 21, 23) sts.

Next Row (Dec Row—RS): Knit across until 3 sts rem, k2tog, k1—20 (20, 20, 22) sts.

Rep Dec Row every RS row 4 more times—16 (16, 16, 18) sts.

Work even until neck measures 2¼", ending after WS row.

Shape Shoulder

Row 1 (RS): BO 6 sts, knit across—10 (10, 10, 12) sts.

Row 2: Purl.

Row 3: BO 5 (5, 5, 6) sts, knit across—5 (5, 5, 6) sts.

Row 4: Purl.

BO.

RIGHT FRONT

Work as for Left Front to Shape Sides.

Shape Sides

Next Row (Dec Row—RS): Knit across until 3 sts rem, k2tog, k1—39 (43, 47, 51) sts.

Rep Dec Row every 18th row 3 more times—36 (40, 44, 48) sts.

Work even until piece measures 17" from beg, ending after RS row.

Shape Armholes

BO 6 (7, 9, 10) sts at beg of next row—30 (33, 35, 38) sts.

Next Row (Dec Row—RS): Knit across until 3 sts rem, k2tog, k1—29 (32, 34, 37) sts.

Rep Dec Row every RS row 4 (6, 7, 8) more times—25 (26, 27, 29) sts.

Work even until armhole measures 6 (7, 7, 8)", ending after WS row.

Shape Neck

BO 4 (5, 6, 6) sts at beg of next row—21 (21, 21, 23) sts.

Next Row: Purl.

Next Row (Dec Row—RS): K1, ssk, knit across—20 (20, 20, 22) sts.

Rep Dec Row every RS row 4 more times—16 (16, 16, 18) sts.

Work even until neck measures 2¼", ending after RS row.

Shape Shoulder

Row 1 (WS): BO 6 sts, purl across—10 (10, 10, 12) sts.

Row 2: Knit.

Row 3: BO 5 (5, 5, 6) sts, purl across—5 (5, 5, 6) sts.

Row 4: Knit.

BO.

SLEEVE (make 2)

Sleeve to Underarm

With smaller needles, CO 42 (44, 50, 54) sts. Beg Broken Rib and work for 2½", ending after RS row.

Dec 6 (6, 8, 8) sts evenly on next row—36 (38, 42, 46) sts. (Use k2tog decrease.)

Change to larger needles, beg Stockinette St and work even until piece measures 3" from beg, ending after WS row.

Next Row (Inc Row—RS): K1, M1 Right, knit across until 1 st rem, M1 Left, k1—38 (40, 44, 48) sts.

Work Inc Row every 4th row 5 (8, 7, 7) more times, then every 6th row 6 (4, 5, 5) times—60 (64, 68, 72) sts.

Work even until piece measures 15 (15, 15½, 15½)" from beg, ending after WS row.

Shape Cap

BO 6 (7, 9, 10) sts at beg of next 2 rows—48 (50, 50, 52) sts.

Next Row (Dec Row—RS): K1, ssk, knit across until 3 sts rem, k2tog, k1—46 (48, 48, 50) sts.

Rep Dec Row every 4th row 1 (3, 4, 6) more times, then every other row 13 (12, 11, 10) times—18 sts.

BO.

FINISHING

Weave in all ends.

Block pieces to measurements.

Sew shoulder seams.

Sew seams to attach sleeves to body.

Sew side seams and sleeve seams.

Neck Edging

With RS facing and circular needle, beg at top right front edge, pick up and knit 62 (66, 70, 70) sts evenly along neck edge. Beg Broken Rib and work for 2½". BO in patt.

Left Front Edging

With RS facing and circular needle, beg at top left front edge, pick up and knit 114 (118, 118, 122) sts evenly along left front edge. Work Broken Rib as follows:

Row 1 (WS): Knit.

Row 2: K1, *k1, p1; rep from * to last st, k1.

Rep Rows 1 and 2 until edging measures 2½" (17 rows total in Broken Rib).

BO in patt.

Right Front Edging

Place markers for three buttonholes on right front edge. Place first marker 1" from top edge. Place bottom marker 5" below first marker. Place third marker evenly between those two.

With RS facing and circular needle, beg at bottom right front edge, pick up and knit 114 (118, 118, 122) sts evenly along right front edge. Work as for Left Front Edging, working buttonholes at markers on 8th row.

Sew buttons to sweater on Left Front opposite buttonholes.

TIP:

To seam the Broken Rib edging so the pattern is not interrupted, use the Invisible Seam on Reverse Stockinette Stitch technique. Ignore the Stockinette Stitch selvage stitches (the edge stitches), and sew into the purl stitches next to the selvage stitches.

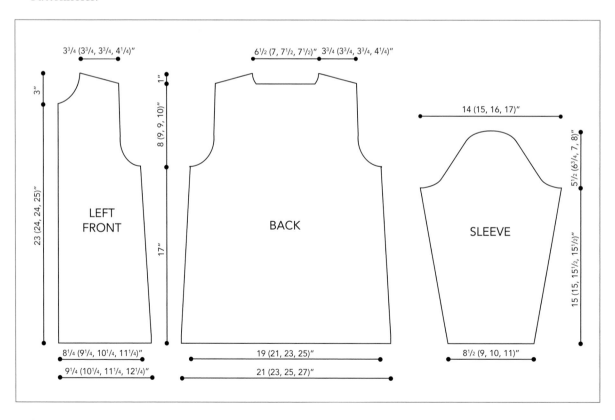

Appendix A

Knitting Abbreviations and Terms Used in This Book

beg
begin(ning)

BO, BO in patt
work in the stitch pattern as you bind off the stitches

BO knitwise
knit the stitches as you bind them off

BO purlwise
purl the stitches as you bind them off

CO
cast on

cont
continue

dec(s)
decrease(s)

dpn(s)
double-pointed needle(s)

estab
established

finished measurement
the measurement of the completed garment as it will be worn; this includes wearing ease and is not the wearer's bust or chest measurement.

g
gram(s)

inc
increase

k
knit

k1 through the back loop
insert right needle from right to left into the back loop of the stitch on the left needle, and knit the stitch (See **through the back loop.**)

k2tog
knit two together (decrease)

knitwise
insert needle into the stitch as if you are knitting

m
meter(s)

M1L, M1 Left
make one left (increase)

M1R, M1 Right
make one right (increase)

mm
millimeter(s)

oz
ounce(s)

p
purl

p2tog
purl two together (decrease)

patt(s)
pattern(s)

purlwise
insert needle into the stitch as if you are purling

rem
remain(s)(ing)

rep
repeat

RS
right side

selvage sts
the first and last stitch on the row. These stitches become the seam allowance when sweater pieces are seamed together. These stitches turn to the wrong side (or inside) of the sweater after the pick-up-and-knit technique has been worked on a vertical or shaped edge.

ssk
slip, slip, knit (decrease)

ssp
slip, slip, purl (decrease)

st(s)
stitch(es)

tbl, through the back loop(s)
insert needle into the back of the loop of the stitch. A stitch on a needle has one loop: the front of that loop is toward the knitter, and the back of that loop is the part of that same stitch that is away from the knitter, on the far side of the needle.

tog
together

work even
continue to work in the stitch pattern without increasing or decreasing

WS
wrong side

yd(s)
yards

Appendix B
Techniques

This section includes cast-on techniques and techniques for seaming the seven sweaters in this book. It also has information about gauge.

Cast Ons

Here is some information about the long-tail cast on and the cable cast on. Both of these cast ons are mentioned in Chapter 1.

Long-Tail Cast On

There are two different ways to make the long-tail cast on. The results are exactly the same in look and structure. The bumpy side of the cast-on edge will be facing the knitter when the knitter works the first row above the cast on edge.

Method 1

This version is found in many knitting books. It is sometimes called the slingshot method.

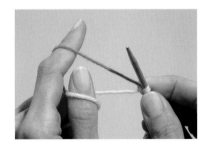

Tie a slip knot in the yarn and place the loop on a knitting needle. Hold the needle in your right hand. In this photo, I am using two different colors of yarn so you can see what is happening. When you do this, use one piece of yarn. The red represents the yarn that goes to the ball; the white is the tail.

Loop the yarn tail (white) around your left thumb. Drape the other yarn (red) over your left index finger.

Insert the right needle into the loop on your thumb.

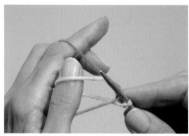

Catch the yarn draped over your index finger with the needle and pull it through the loop.

Remove your thumb from the loop.

Use your left thumb to tighten the yarn. The red stitch has been cast on.

Method 2

I prefer this method because I find it easier to control the tension of the yarn. It is sometimes referred to as the thumb method. Again, I am using two different colors of yarn so you can see what is happening. When you do this, use one piece of yarn. The red represents the yarn that goes to the ball; the white is the tail.

Tie a slip knot in the yarn and place the loop on a knitting needle. Hold the needle in your right hand. Loop the yarn tail (white) around the left thumb. Hold the other yarn (red) in the right hand.

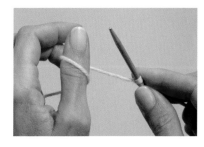

Insert the needle into the loop.

With your right hand, bring the yarn around the right needle as if you are knitting a stitch. (I have to grab the needle with my left thumb and index finger when I do this; if I don't, the needle falls out of my right hand.)

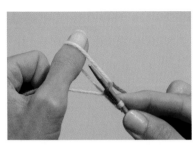

Pull the right needle through the loop on your left thumb.

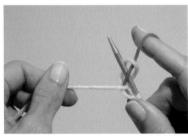

Remove your thumb from the loop and tighten the yarn by pulling the tail in your left hand.

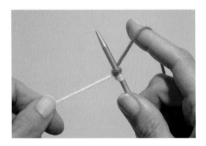

The red stitch has been cast on.

Cable Cast On

The cable cast on technique is covered in Chapter 7 because it is used in the one-row horizontal buttonhole. The smooth side of the cast-on edge will be facing the knitter when the knitter works the first row above the cast-on edge.

Seams

Sew all of these seams with the RS facing. Thread yarn through a tapestry needle. Use the sweater yarn if it is appropriate for seaming. In these pictures, the seams are sewn with a contrasting color of yarn so you can see what is happening.

Tip: In the first five seam techniques, the tapestry needle always enters the fabric at the place where the yarn came out of the fabric previously.

Invisible Seam on Stockinette Stitch—Mattress Stitch

Use this technique to sew vertical seams like side seams and sleeve seams from the wrist to the underarm.

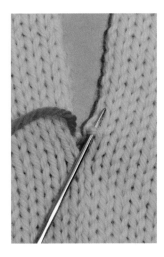

With the knit side (RS) facing you,

1. Insert the tapestry needle under the horizontal running thread between the first and second stitches on one side. Then, insert the tapestry needle under the horizontal running thread between the first and second stitches on the other side.

2. Continue to alternate from one side to the other, tightening the sewing yarn every fourth or fifth stitch.

Invisible Seam on Reverse Stockinette Stitch

Use this technique to sew vertical seams.

With the purl side (RS) facing you,

1. Insert the needle into the top loop (purl nub) inside the edge on one side.

2. Then insert the needle into the bottom loop of the corresponding stitch inside the edge on the other side.

3. Continue to alternate from one side (sewing under top loops) to the other side (sewing under bottom loops), tightening the sewing yarn every fourth or fifth stitch.

K1 P1 Ribbing

Add knit stitches to both edges of the ribbing, and use them as selvage stitches.

Knit the ribbing as follows: Row 1(RS): K1, *k1, p1; rep from *, end k1. Row 2: P1, *k1, p1; rep from *, end p1. With the right side facing you, sew the seam on the left side as for invisible seam on stockinette stitch. Sew the seam on the right side as for invisible seam on reverse stockinette stitch, skipping the edge stitch and sewing into the purl stitch. Insert the needle into bottom loop that is closest to the edge.

Invisible Horizontal Seam

Use this technique to sew shoulder seams.

Sew this seam from right to left with the right side facing you.

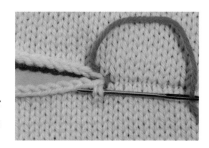

1. On the bottom piece, bring the tapestry needle through the center of the first stitch inside the bound-off edge. Bring the needle from the back of the fabric to the front.

2. On the top piece, insert the needle under one stitch inside the bound-off edge.

3. On the bottom piece, insert the needle into the center of the same stitch worked previously and then bring the needle out of the center of the next stitch to the left.

4. On the top piece, insert the needle under the next stitch, inserting the needle at the same place where the yarn came out of the fabric previously.

5. Repeat steps 3 and 4 to sew the seam.

6. Tighten the sewing yarn in this seam.

Invisible Horizontal-to-Vertical Seam

Use this seam to join the top of the sleeve (bound-off edge of stitches) to the garment body (rows of stitches). This is a combination of the invisible horizontal seam (here, sewn on the sleeve edge) and the invisible seam on stockinette stitch (also called mattress stitch; here, sewn on the body edge).

Sew this seam from right to left with the right side facing you.

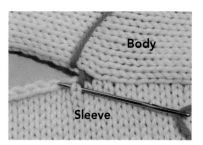

1. On the sleeve, bring the tapestry needle through the center of the first stitch inside the bound-off edge. Bring the needle from the back of the fabric to the front.

2. Insert the needle under a horizontal running thread on the body, as in the invisible seam on stockinette stitch.

3. Insert the needle into the center of the same stitch worked previously in the sleeve piece and then bring needle out of the center of the next stitch to the left.

4. Repeat steps 2 and 3 to sew the seam.

5. Be sure to reconcile the row gauge to the stitch gauge by working under two running threads on the body occasionally.

6. Tighten the sewing yarn in this seam.

Three-Needle Bind Off—"Knitting the Shoulders Together"

This technique is used to join shoulders, but it does not involve sewing. Use yarn that matches the sweater.

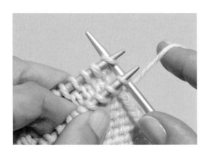

1. Place the shoulder stitches on two needles. Place the needles side by side with the right sides of the fabric together and the needles pointing in the same direction. Hold these needles in your left hand with the tips pointing to the right.

2. Insert a third needle (held in your right hand) knitwise into the first stitch on each needle and wrap the yarn around the needle as if to knit.

3. Knit the two stitches together and slip them off the needles.

4. Knit the next two stitches together in the same way.

5. With one of the left needles, slip the second stitch from the tip on the right-hand needle over the first stitch (next to the tip) on the right-hand needle and drop it off the needle. (In other words, bind off one stitch.)

6. Repeat steps 4 and 5 until all stitches have been bound off.

Tips on Sewing Seams to Attach Sleeves

For the garments with modified drop shoulders (Diamond Yoke Pullover and Two-Texture Pullover), use the invisible horizontal-to-vertical seam to attach the sleeve to the body.

For the garments with set-in sleeves (Baby Cardi, Eugenie's Cardigan, Color Tie Cardigan, and My Sister's Sweater), use three different seaming techniques in different places:

- To sew together the bound-off underarm areas of the sleeve and the body, use the invisible horizontal seam.

- To attach the vertical sections of the sleeve to the body, use the invisible seam on stockinette stitch (also called mattress stitch).

- To attach the bound-off edge at the top of the sleeve to the body (in the shoulder area), use the invisible horizontal-to-vertical seam.

Gauge

If you care about the fit of a sweater you plan to make, work a gauge swatch. Patterns assume the knitter will achieve a certain number of stitches and rows per inch, and the sizing of the garment is based on that. For example, if the sweater pattern tells you that the gauge is 6 stitches to the inch, but you get only 5 stitches to the inch, that sweater, which is supposed to have a 36-inch chest measurement, will actually have a 43-inch chest measurement. This is a difference of approximately two sweater sizes.

To obtain an accurate gauge measurement, knit a large swatch in the stitch pattern specified, using the sweater yarn and the needles you plan to use for the sweater. The swatch should be a minimum of 4 inches by 4 inches, but the bigger the swatch, the more accurate the gauge measurement. I like to make swatches that are 8 inches by 8 inches.

When you calculate gauge, be sure to measure a significant portion of the swatch. For stitch gauge, measure across most of the swatch, but don't include the first or last stitch on the row because these stitches can be larger and loopier than all the other stitches in the row. Divide the number of stitches by the number of inches to determine the number of stitches per inch for your swatch.

For example, if 35 stitches are in a 7-inch measurement, then 35 stitches divided by 7 inches is 5 stitches per inch. If you do not get the specified gauge, change the needle size, knit another swatch, and measure again. This sounds tedious, but it will ensure that you knit a sweater that turns out to be the size you want.

If you change to a larger needle, the stitches will be more spread out, and the gauge will have fewer stitches per inch. If you get a gauge of 5 stitches per inch with needles of a certain size, using larger-size needles will spread out the stitches and move your gauge in the direction of 4 stitches per inch. Likewise, with smaller-size needles, the stitches will be closer together and the gauge will have more stitches per inch, moving your gauge closer to 6 stitches per inch.

For row gauge, the process is basically the same except you need to measure vertically in the swatch and count the number of rows. But keep in mind that for sweaters knit from the bottom to the top (not side to side) stitch gauge will be more important than row gauge. Sweater patterns almost always allow for variances in row gauge by instructing the knitter to "work even until piece measures x inches." So your piece will be the right length even if your gauge is 5.5 rows per inch and the specified gauge is 6 rows per inch.

Appendix C

Yarns

The following companies provided the yarn for the garments in this book. These companies are wholesalers. Contact them to find retail stores in your area that carry their yarn.

Brown Sheep Company, Inc.
100662 County Road 16
Mitchell, Nebraska 69357
(800) 826-9136
www.brownsheep.com

Cascade Yarns
1224 Andover Park East
Tukwila, Washington 98188-3905
(206) 574-0440
www.cascadeyarns.com

Mission Falls
c/o CNS Yarns
5333 Casgrain #1204
Montreal, QC H2T 1X3 Canada
(877) 244-1204
(514) 276-1204
www.missionfalls.com

Appendix D

Bibliography

A Second Treasury of Knitting Patterns, by Barbara G. Walker. New York: Charles Scribner's Sons, 1970.

Reader's Digest Knitter's Handbook, by Montse Stanley. Pleasantville, N.Y.: Reader's Digest Association, 1993.

The Knitter's Companion, by Vicki Square. Loveland, Colo.: Interweave Press, 1996.

The Master Hand Knitting Program. Zanesville, Ohio: The Knitting Guild Association. I completed the program in the mid 1990s, and the program is ongoing.

The Principles of Knitting: Methods and Techniques of Hand Knitting, by June Hemmons Hiatt. New York: Simon and Schuster, 1988.

Vogue Knitting: The Ultimate Knitting Book, by The Editors of Vogue Knitting Magazine. New York: Pantheon Books, 1989.

Some of the books in my personal collection (left) have been reissued as newer editions since I bought mine:

A Second Treasury of Knitting Patterns, by Barbara G. Walker. Pittsville, Wisc.: Schoolhouse Press, 1998.

The Knitter's Companion, by Vicki Square. Loveland, Colo.: Interweave Press, 2006.

Vogue Knitting: The Ultimate Knitting Book, by The Editors of Vogue Knitting Magazine. New York: Sixth & Spring Books, 2002.

Appendix E
Resources

For information about knitting and knitting groups, and to find out about the Master Hand Knitting Program, contact:

The Knitting Guild Association
1100-H Brandywine Boulevard
Zanesville, OH 43701
(740) 452-4541
www.tkga.com
tkga@tkga.com